GLOBAL CAREER:

HOW TO WORK ANYWHERE AND TRAVEL FOREVER

Michael T. Swigunski

Ross,

You truly are the
Ping-Pong champ!

Mike Swigunski

Global Career:
How to Work Anywhere and Travel Forever

This book is designed to provide information that the author believes to be accurate on the subject matter it covers, and is written from the author's personal experience.

Any references to resources and materials produced by other entities are purely the author's own interpretation. The author does not imply an endorsement from any of the sources cited within this book.

ISBN 978-1-7326230-4-0 (*Kindle*)

ISBN 978-1-7326230-1-9 (*Print*)

First Printing, 2018

New Nomad Publishing

globalcareerbook.com

Interior Design: Annabel Brandon

To my mom, Fran Swigunski, who passed away from breast cancer on April 18, 2011.

"Carry my love east to west. Wherever you go I'll go too … love knows no distance or time." —Mom

CONTENTS

Acknowledgments

Chapter 1: Introduction — 1
Work to Live or Live to Work? — 1
A Life of Both Working and Traveling Really Is Possible — 5
The Shorter Path — 7
The Low-Hanging Fruits — 10
Why Me (Why I'm the Expert) — 12
What Is a Global Career? — 16
What You're Going to Learn — 19
About Me: Who Is Michael Swigunski? — 22

Chapter 2: Studying Abroad — 29
My Experience Studying Abroad — 29
Going for It — 35
Facing Challenges — 44
Another Study Abroad Option – Semester at Sea — 49
Benefits, Both Professional and Personal — 50
Coming Back Home — 55

Chapter 3: Interning Abroad — 59
My Experience as an Intern — 61
Opportunities — 66
Benefits — 68
International Internships Broaden Your Future's Horizons — 71
Apprenticeships — 73
Finding and Preparing for an International Internship — 74

Chapter 4, VOL. I: Working Abroad 79

Intro 79

Getting Started 84

Once You're There, the Initiation 88

Transitioning to Build Your Career 93

Final Thoughts 97

Chapter 4, VOL. II: Working Abroad 99

Options and Opportunities 99

Working Holiday Visa (WHV) 101

Visa Options for Travelers over Thirty 118

Examples of Non-Working Visas around the World 119

Remote Work or Freelancing Online 125

Large International Organizations (Accenture, P&G, EY, etc.) with Offices Worldwide 126

Working on a Cruise Ship 127

ESL + Transition to Another Career 127

Volunteer or WWOOFing 128

Conclusion 129

Chapter 5: The Expat Life 131

Intro 131

Becoming a Community Member 133

Facing Expat Challenges 136

Becoming an Expert Expat 138

Crossing Your T's and Dotting Your I's 140

Final Thoughts on the Expat Life 143

Chapter 6: Travel Tips 145
Intro 145
Banking, Credit Cards, Spending 147
Travel Insurance 156
Transportation 158
Resources 160
Networking 163
Phone and Internet 165
Packing Tips 166
Conclusion 172

Chapter 7: Afterword: My Final Thoughts 175
From Novice to Expert 180
Want Some Help? 183

Inspiration 185

Resources 195

I like to keep a list of all the countries I have visited and all all of the other places I dream of going to in the future. It's both an aspirational list, and a reminder of the great times I've had throughout my global career, and something I'd encourage everyone to do. In the lower margins of every page are lists of countries waiting to be checked off. I would suggest using this space to also keep track of some of your favorite memories, like "Visited Oktoberfest in Germany and drank beer with the Mayor of Germany in 2016." Writing down your favorite experience or memory will be something you can cherish when reminiscing about your past travels! Better yet, it could even be a local person's contact information you met while traveling in that specific country. This is your portion of the book, so feel free to use it however you like!

☑ IRELAND

Visited my Irish friend, Adrian O'Higgins, in Dublin for St. Patrick's day in 2012.

☐ AFGHANISTAN

ALBANIA

ACKNOWLEDGMENTS

This wild journey of working and traveling would not have been possible without the tremendous amount of support from family, friends, and mentors. There are so many people to acknowledge who have supported me over the years.

I would like to start by expressing my deepest gratitude to my family members. None of this would have been possible without the never-ending love and guidance from my mom, dad, brother, and the rest of my extended family. You have been there for me every step of the way (literally) from when I was born to current day. You've instilled values that I am forever grateful for and taught me that anything is possible.

To my girlfriend, Alejandra, thanks so much for supporting me every step of the way. You have been by my side all across the world, and I am so grateful to have you in my life. You have been extremely helpful in every aspect of my life, and I can't wait to see the rest of the world together!

To my friends—thanks for putting up with me over the years and for always being there for me, in the good times and the bad. We have created some amazing memories close to home and all across the world. Here's to more adventures and some of the best friends a guy could ask for.

To my mentors: Chuck, Professor Ferris, Ki, Justin, and Joe. You all have played tremendously important roles as mentors for me. Each one of you has helped me get to where I am now in my career, and you have each been a big inspiration for this book.

To all the amazing people I've met along the way. Throughout all my travels, I have crossed paths with so many incredible, friendly, generous, and just all-around great people. The world truly is an astonishing place filled with astounding people.

XIII

ANGOLA

CHAPTER 1:

INTRODUCTION

Work to Live or Live to Work?

This book is about how to travel *as a way of life*—for years, if you want. I'll talk about how to find work and build a career, study abroad, or move for work, all while pursuing your passion for seeing the world.

I'll describe myself in more detail further on in this chapter, but for now I just want to say that if you're looking for proof of concept that living and traveling abroad can work, I offer myself as a pretty good example of what you can accomplish. My own work and travel history contains a vast array of experiences, from frugal budget trips to some pretty luxurious travels.

To say that I've worked a wide variety of jobs would be an understatement. I've taught financial economics at the Czech University in Prague, worked for startups in Australia and New Zealand, interned for a political party in Ireland, worked the Wells Fargo trading floor in the US, and even did some modeling in Korea. I currently work a remote, online marketing job for an American company called Empire Flippers. If someone had told me years ago that I could earn over six figures without having to step into an office, I would have thought it was a joke. I used to think those types of opportunities were only available for experienced developers. But that's my reality.

Studying abroad introduced me to the idea of living and working overseas. I took a summer course in Bergamo, Italy, and completed a two-year fully funded MBA in South Korea. One of my first international jobs was working with the University of Missouri's study abroad program, organizing and managing study abroad sessions in Prague.

When it comes to traveling, the accommodation experiences alone are amazing. I've stayed in 10,000-square-foot villas. At the other end of the spectrum, while attending the Running of the Bulls in Pamplona, I slept in a park (sans tent) for three days. I've done what's expected of budget-conscious travelers—Couch Surfing, Airbnb, hostels. I've also stayed at five-star hotels and resorts and on private yachts. I've taken cruises, and I've traveled on small Thai long-tail boats. I hitchhiked for a month, and I've driven a Tesla in Miami. There is truly no perfect way to travel, and you'll slowly be able to find out what works and what's sustainable.

It's not my intent to brag about how special I am or that my experience is exceptional. It's actually the opposite—I believe that with determination and passion, anyone can replicate the same kind of freedom and success that I have. *You* can have it. Wouldn't that be amazing?

With this book, I want to show everyone that living and working abroad can be fantastic—not only emotionally empowering and fulfilling, but also a very good career move.

I think this is the best time in history for people to explore living and traveling abroad. Remote work is becoming increasingly common. More and more of us are working from home (or wherever we want!) in jobs that don't require us to report to an office every day. Study abroad programs are becoming even more common, so young people are traveling all over the world while finishing their degrees. It is becoming more and more possible to make traveling a long-term part of your life, something you do for a year or two (or five) at a time, instead of the two-week vacation most Americans are accustomed to.

We all have that friend of a friend who backpacked through Europe for six months, or who's a "digital nomad" (someone who can work anywhere with an internet connection—they're easily spotted in the wild at your local Starbucks), or who lives and works overseas. And it can sometimes seem like it's something other people can do, but not us. That kind of thing is for people with more money, or with the right kind of job, or who are at the right time in their lives (before kids, before owning a home, etc.). I think Americans, in particular, don't always see traveling for years as something that's attainable. We tend to see it as a gap in our real life; you go backpacking for a summer, then come back and get a real job. Traveling, for Americans, is like taking a break from reality. You're not earning money, you're not pushing your career forward. You're having a great time, but it's momentary; your career is stagnating.

But it doesn't have to be that way. I'm here to show you that if you want to travel as a lifestyle, if you want to work abroad, or get a global degree, or do something resume-worthy while seeing the world, you absolutely can.

Lots of people do, and I can help you figure out exactly how to make it work.

There are opportunities out there for anyone, whether you have an established career and want to work overseas as a contractor, or you're just out of high school and want to study in another country. The thing is, these opportunities are always out there—but if you're not looking, or you think traveling isn't for you, you're probably going to miss them.

If you want travel to be a core aspect of your life, and to make a good living while you explore the world, you can. In this book, I am going to show you how to recognize the opportunities that appear all around you—and how to take advantage of them so you can turn your dreams into reality.

A Life of Both Working and Traveling Really Is Possible

Growing up in St. Louis, Missouri, I always knew about the classic life plan. We'll call it Plan A:

- Step 1: After high school, attend college and earn a degree.

- Step 2: Get a good job in your field of study, work hard, save money, and retire.

- Options: Fit travel into your two weeks of annual vacation time, and go on a cruise or two when you retire.

Of course, we all know this isn't the only way to live your life, but I want to show that long-term traveling—traveling as a lifestyle—is a very real alternative. People like me are doing it happily and successfully, right now!

I currently work for an online business brokerage, and my job title is Marketing and Sales Coordinator. Overall, I suppose I identify as a digital nomad, but I feel more like a "Location Independent Professional." I don't report to a brick-and-mortar office; all my work is done online. And I make a great living.

My industry is marketing, and the company I work for helps people generate income by purchasing online businesses. The businesses they purchase generate a steady and profitable income that they can use to support their other goals. It's like an alternative investment strategy.

It's a slightly higher risk, but it generates a much higher reward. In a way, my work kind of reflects my life—where I'm taking an alternate path, but one that is a completely viable option.

I've developed this career over many years. I tried a few different fields, like finance and teaching, and found they weren't for me. So it was a process to find this lifestyle, where I can travel while working remotely, but now I can show others that it is completely possible. It might sound too good to be true, but it isn't. It's completely doable.

The Shorter Path

This book presents all the shortcuts, tools, and tips that I learned the hard way—and that I wish I had known when I was starting out. I figured it all out eventually, but it took me five years to get set up in the type of online career I always dreamed of, and it didn't need to take that long. If I had known when I started out that there was plenty of remote work out there that would pay a good wage and support my travel (or whatever else I wanted to do with my life), I would have gone straight for that. I used to think that online jobs were available only for experienced programmers, but there are opportunities in any field!

But I still had traditional perceptions about what kind of work I needed based on the "Plan A" aspirations that I started off with, and those held me back longer than they needed to. I created this book to help you learn about all the options available when it comes to work and travel so you don't spend too much unnecessary time doing something that simply won't help you reach your long-term goals.

This is not to say that whatever path you've taken in life wasn't worth it. Even if an opportunity didn't work out or wasn't what you wanted, if you learned from it and moved forward, it was valuable.

But there are some opportunities in life that have a "jumping-off point"—you've reached a certain place in your career, and you really need to jump off and move on to the next thing, before you get stuck. For example, I know a lot of people who teach English abroad. Like me with my current job, they got into it because it's a good way to combine traveling and making some money. The difference is,

BAHRAIN

they don't *really* want to teach English. It's not the career they're interested in. And for many of them, it's not even related to what they want to do. Maybe they're interested in graphic design, marketing, or web design. But instead, they're working a job that isn't related to their career goals.

At some point, they realize they've become established as an English teacher, and it would take a lot of work to pivot toward the industry they actually want to be in. They'd have to leave their teaching job and either go back to school or take an entry-level job in the field they want— and go back to making less money to start all over again. I've seen this happen countless times with expats—they take jobs that don't further their career, and when they decide to pivot, they need to start from square one.

I think this happens because people don't realize what opportunities are out there, or they don't have enough information to accurately evaluate what's the best move for them. Like me and remote work, I didn't know how much work there was or what kinds of jobs were available when I started out. I thought remote jobs were only for coders or freelancers. Travel was my number one priority, and work allowed me to do it. So I took whatever types of job I needed to to make my dreams of travel come true.

Teaching ESL (English as a Second Language) is a great way to pay for your travel. And it may be one of the best ways to get your foot in the door in a new country. But unless you want to be an ESL teacher, you should be keeping an eye out for your next opportunity. Sometimes, instead of being on the lookout for that next career move, people stick with teaching because it's what they know. But you don't have to make that trade-off. You don't have to settle for a job that's irrelevant to your career path just to make money for traveling. You can make money doing a job you like and that will further your career path, *and* you can travel.

Another limiting belief many people fall victim to is that they'll be all on their own in a new country. They won't know anyone, and there will be no one to help if they need something. It's a valid concern that can hold people back, whether it's conscious or subconscious. This is a gross misconception. There are expat communities in every country, and you can easily find them online or with numerous other tactics. There will be people just like you (sometimes lots of them) in whatever city or town you're in who are new to that country, and they'll be looking to make friends with others who are in the same boat. You can build your own community pretty quickly, if you set out to do that, and take those connections with you anywhere you go.

And it's not like there isn't a cost to staying put. Studies show that people tend to regret the things they didn't do, even more and longer than they regret the things they did. There's even a term for it: inaction regret. In other words, chances are that if think you'd like to live abroad and don't at least give it a try, you will regret *not* having done it a lot more, and longer, than you would regret trying it and having it not work out for you. That's a significant cost that people should seriously consider as they're contemplating something like this. In American culture, we tend to think, "I'll do it later—when I'm retired." But you never know what could come up later in life to keep you from traveling. If you have the desire to travel *now*, you should travel now. Why not?

The Low-Hanging Fruits

There are opportunities to work and travel all over the place, but it helps if you know where to look—and that's what this book is for.

For example, there are countries where it's very easy for Americans to get work visas. In some places, like Australia, you can even do it all online. Then you can show up in that country and work practically any job that a native-born citizen could do. That's an amazing opportunity right there, and a lot of people don't know about it. You can easily get a work visa in Ireland, South Korea, New Zealand, Australia, and Singapore. Sometimes they have a requirement that you must have a few thousand dollars in your bank account, but it's not more than what you would need to move there anyway. For New Zealand, for example, it is around US$3,000.

You can start exploring opportunities right now, without changing anything else in your life. The easiest way to start your journey is to pick one of the countries I've just listed, go online, and look at applying for a visa. Once you have it, you can start applying for jobs.

I always moved to the country and applied in person. If that feels too risky, you can apply for jobs online and set things up so a job is waiting for you when you arrive. Another option is to arrange for an extended visit to the country. That way, you can apply for jobs in person and test the waters before you make a permanent move.

One of the truths that I can share from my experience, which you might not have thought of if you haven't lived abroad and traveled yourself, is how similar all the processes are at the end of the day. We tend to assume it will be massively complicated—getting a visa will be hard, job hunting will be difficult, everything will be different, you won't know how to do things. But the basic principles are the same everywhere. If you know how to look for work in the United States, you can apply that knowledge directly to the international job market and look for the same kind of jobs you'd look for at home. Or, of course, you can find a remote job that you can work online—like I (eventually) did.

This is a huge part of the message of this book: working, traveling, and living abroad is a completely viable way to live. One of the greatest results I've seen from trying to spread the word about traveling long term is from a blog post I wrote about moving to New Zealand with less than $3,000. I saw comments on that post saying, "Wow, I didn't even know this was a possibility. Thanks for your blog post. I'm going to move to New Zealand." That's incredibly satisfying—to know I helped someone see that open door and walk through it. And now I want to spread the word even more.

Work visas, and even tourist visas, can get really complicated, so I decided to create an easy-to-use tool that simplifies the process. You can access the free tool here: globalcareerbook.com/visas.

Why Me (Why I'm the Expert)

I was born in St. Louis, Missouri, and I didn't take my first international flight until I was around eighteen. International travel wasn't a big part of my life growing up. So if I can do it, anyone can.

I got my first taste for travel when I went to Europe with my brother and father. I saw a lot of Italy, and I loved it. After I came back to the States and started college, my roommate and I decided we wanted to study in Italy the next summer. We made it happen, and those six weeks were enough to make me think, "I want to do this more. What are my options?" So already, you can see a bit of a progression. I started off just wanting to see one country that I already knew a bit (Italy), and that developed into loving the idea of travel in general—and wanting to find ways to do a lot more of it.

One of the student managers of that study abroad program suggested to me that I would be a good fit as a study abroad student manager (what she was doing) and that I should apply. It was a two-year internship, working for the university as their student manager for a particular city. I got the job, and they assigned me to the Prague program. I had different duties throughout the year. For the first semester, I worked with marketing and prep work. For the second semester, I taught a university course for predeparture. In the summer, I was the student manager in Prague, worked as a teaching assistant for a professor, helped with logistics, and performed other various duties.

For my second (and last) summer in Prague, I decided to book a one-way flight instead of a round trip and see if I could find a job that could keep me there after the internship was done. And the rest was history. I've described my life story in full, in the About Me section at the end of this chapter, to use my life as an example of what it really looks like to go from being someone with ordinary goals and aspirations to someone who lives and works abroad (and loves it!).

By this point, I'd seen firsthand how my personal passion for travel could directly feed into my global career goals and help me accomplish things that I never could have done if I had just stayed in the United States.

I started traveling pretty much full time when I was twenty-one, when most people are starting their careers and going through all the angst about what job they want, how to get it, and whether it will pay enough. I went through all the same angst but as a traveler, and I learned a surprising truth: traveling can be very good for your career.

Traveling doesn't just have to happen in the background of your career. It can be something that directly feeds your career and helps you get where you want to be. I'm a big believer in making things happen for yourself. If you want to get into a particular industry and you don't have experience, there are ways to create that experience or find an opening for yourself. Just think about all the people you meet traveling, and all the one-of-a-kind opportunities you could hear about or be in the right place at the right time for.

As an example, I've gained attention online with my travel blog, where I talk about the lessons I've learned and the best ways to travel and work. I wrote a blog post about how I moved to Australia with a small amount of money, and it blew up. I built my own website for the blog, and I was able to use that as an example of my online business knowledge to get my current job.

Here's another example: While working at a university in Prague, I met a professor who worked at a university in Gwangju, South Korea. I saw him as a mentor, and we kept in touch over the next few years. He told me about an MBA scholarship opportunity, so I spent weeks on the application and got it. Thanks to traveling, hard work, and networking, I was able to get my MBA (for free), and I got the opportunity to spend a few years in South Korea, which was an amazing experience.

What I love about working and traveling is that there are so many ways to do it. When I started working abroad, I was actually looking for a conventional office job, but just in another country. I did start off working jobs like that, but over time I realized that I wanted to work in a way that would support my traveling, instead of my travel getting squeezed into my vacation time from my real job.

After a few years, I started transitioning toward remote work. Now, for a lot of people, working a regular job in another country is exactly what they want. That's great if it suits you best, but my point is that you can do more than that (or less than that) if you want to, and you don't even have to commit to one or the other. You can start in one place, in one type of job, and then transition toward wherever it is you really want to be, when and as you figure that out.

This book will inform you about all your options right off the bat and provide you with a head start to success. With the information I provide, you can figure it out even faster. It's a five-year shortcut, which I can't wait to share!

The thing about working and traveling is that once you

start doing it, you become more flexible; your whole life becomes a little more "portable." You've already done the hard work of leaving behind your "Plan A" life, if you had one. Once you've done that, if you're contemplating any other kind of life change needed to get the job you want—like going back to school or moving somewhere else for an opportunity—it's a lot easier to think about, because you've already done it. The working/traveling life can support your career goals by putting you in a position where you're willing and able to make the changes you need to get the life you want.

I think most of the barriers to living and traveling, for those who want to, are mental barriers. There are logistic issues, like figuring out the paperwork. But like I said, that stuff is pretty easy to figure out once you decide to go and look at it. What most people are up against is a sort of vague, "Oh, this isn't the right time," or "I don't know, maybe it will be really hard, maybe I'll screw something up" kind of feeling.

I know that if you really want the working and traveling life, you can figure out how to do it. I also know that some people need to see that *it can be done* before they can muster the motivation to make it happen for themselves. And this book—which lays out exactly how to do it—gives you the tips and tools to make it easier, and shows you a true success story (mine): you can jump over that mental hurdle of believing the life you want isn't attainable for you.

What Is a Global Career?

In essence, this book is intended to reframe your perceptions of what it takes to work and travel overseas. I want to convince you that not only is it possible to travel for years, as a way of life, but that you don't have to give up your career aspirations to do it. In fact, working and traveling can be great for your career. Whether you find the work you're looking for overseas and stay there or you return to the United States at some point, you will have job experience that is not only relevant, but also says something about you as a person. It says you're resourceful, versatile, and agile. You can think outside the box. You can create an opportunity for yourself where others wouldn't have seen an opportunity at all.

Whether it's overseas work experience, an internship, or an international degree, that experience becomes a talking point on your resume. It makes you a little more interesting than other candidates, a little more memorable to the recruiter or interviewer. And those little things can give you a serious edge.

It's a very competitive job market out there, and the bar is getting pushed higher. It's not enough to have some volunteer experience or an internship on your resume, so something like having worked a job in another country can be the perfect way to differentiate yourself.

And it's not only work experience. As a traveler, you encounter tons of different people and situations. You have to think on your feet and get used to looking at things from another cultural perspective. That kind of personal growth gives you a lot more empathy and confidence as an individual, and that will help you with all your life goals, whether they're career related or not.

I also want to show that this is not an expensive way to live. People think, "Oh, I'll need to save up a lot of money or win the lottery before I can go traveling." That's another misconception. There are ways to travel very cheaply, doing things like couch surfing (where you find people online who will let you stay in their home). WWOOFing (World Wide Opportunities on Organic Farms) is another option many people find interesting. Through the organization, you find people online who will let you stay and work with them on their farm, so you get to learn all about sustainable agriculture while living in Greece or Ireland, for example. There are tons of international communities out there, all built around a passion or an interest, where people will network and help each other out. You just need to find yours. In a lot of situations, you can actually save more money living abroad since you can earn in US dollars and spend in the local currency.

Traveling as a way of life is not like taking a vacation. It's not time off from your real life. It *is* your real life, and you can keep growing your career, or working toward any other goals you may have, while you do it. Not only that, but international travel will expose you to so many new ideas, so many different ways of life, that you'll be inspired to find a way of life that works for you.

In this book, I want to show that you can achieve your dream; not just the American dream of the nine-to-five job, but *your* actual dream—how you really want to live and work. Most of us don't know exactly what that is when we start out, but I'll show you how traveling and working abroad for years can help you figure that out and make it happen.

BOTSWANA

I believe that we are starting to see a cultural shift toward the kind of life that I lead, and that others lead, where work and life look completely different from what our parents had. I want to spread the word about this transition that's taking place, and help it grow, so that more and more people are living and working on *their* terms and pursuing their personal goals at the same time.

Right now, remote work and long-term traveling are like the "unicorns" of work; everyone's heard of this lifestyle, but they've never actually experienced it themselves. It's always a friend of a friend or someone you know telling you about it, but you've never tried it yourself. I want to show that this can be *a normal way to live*. It can be a lifestyle that isn't particularly special. A lifestyle that doesn't need a book written about it, because it's become the "new normal" for so many people.

What You're Going to Learn

In this book, I'll cover:

- How to efficiently find work you actually want

- The best and easiest ways to get your paperwork in order and move overseas

- Advice on treating this time as a transitional time for your career by exploring new options that are in line with your goals

- Practical ways to find accommodations, what kinds of living expenses to expect, etc.

- Steps to set up a life where you can travel while studying, doing an internship, or working abroad, all in the interests of your long-term career goals

The chapters of this book follow a progression, much like the progression I followed as I got into traveling and working, or the one you might follow as you get started:

Chapter 2 covers studying abroad—the easiest way to dip your toe into travel if you're still in college, with options lasting anywhere from two weeks to a year.

Chapter 3 covers doing an internship abroad—this gets you work experience, and it's a longer-term option (a few months, or a year).

Chapter 4 covers full-time work overseas—the key point here is: anything you would be doing in the United States, you can do overseas.

I'll also discuss remote work, because in my opinion this is the best and fastest way to accomplish your career goals alongside your personal goal of freedom to travel. I slowly transitioned into remote work, but you can go straight for it, now that you know it's a viable option. This kind of work will give you the most freedom and ability to configure your life however you want. There are jobs that function like a nine-to-five, but just in a home office instead of a corporate office. There are also jobs, like mine, that are task-based—as long as you accomplish whatever you're supposed to and deliver your work on time, *when* you work doesn't matter. These jobs come with KPIs (Key Performance Indicators) or weekly goals to help keep you on track, but they allow you to structure your "workday" however you want.

And with remote work, you can still work for an American company—from wherever in the world you want to be. This is also where you'll see that if you want to transition to a new industry, you can do that abroad, using your existing education and experience as a basis to pivot from.

Chapter 5 looks at life as an expat—what to expect and how to find expat communities (or build one) in the countries you live in.

Chapter 6 provides all sorts of travel tips—what you need to pack, how to find appropriate living accommodations, and aspects you've probably never considered.

Chapter 7 wraps up the package—a final look at the ideas, tips, and tools provided in previous chapters, and encouragement to follow your work and travel lifestyle dreams.

This book is for anyone who dreams of having a lifestyle of working and traveling around the world. You might have just finished college and are starting to look at the next step on your "Plan A" life path. If you're starting to go to interviews and none of the companies sound that great, this book might be for you. Or if you have a "real job" already, and you've been doing it for a few years and you thought by now you'd enjoy it, but you still don't, this book might be for you. Or you might have a long-standing career but feel stuck, longing for the day you can leave the day-to-day grind and live your dream of seeing the world.

What this book will do for you is turn your dream of traveling "one day" into something imminent, something you know you can do, right now. Instead of idly looking up vacation destinations for that trip you want to take someday, I want to get you looking up flight times, finding the website to submit your visa application, and posting on social media asking if your friends know anyone in New Zealand—or wherever it is in the world that you want to see.

About Me: Who Is Michael Swigunski?

This is the story of my life and how I got into living and traveling abroad. I'm using this as a case study to show that it can be done by anyone. I had a pretty ordinary, American childhood and adolescence, and if I can end up with this amazing, alternative life that I didn't even know existed until a few years ago, you can too.

I was born in 1988 in St. Louis, Missouri. My dad was an electrical engineer and my mom was an accountant, but when my brother and I were born, she left her job to stay home with us. I have a brother I am really close with, and we are great friends. He's a talented musician and biomedical engineer. My parents didn't take us around the world as kids. As I mentioned earlier, the first time I took an international flight was when I was around the age of eighteen, and my brother was twenty-two. There was nothing special that made it so I would love travel—nothing that anyone else couldn't replicate.

I graduated from Lafayette High School in 2007 and decided to study finance at the University of Missouri the following year. That summer, my dad took me and my brother to Europe. We saw Italy, France, Monaco, and London. As I said earlier, that was when I started to love travel; I got to see a lot of Italy and really wanted to go back.

The next year, I went back to Italy as part of my university's study abroad program. We studied in Italy, but I managed to squeeze in trips to Spain, Munich, London, and Paris. I had a wonderful time studying and traveling. I was ready for more, but I also was ready to return home for a while and spend time with my family.

The family time I was looking forward to did not end up being what I had envisioned. Shortly after my return to the United States, my mom was diagnosed with stage 4 breast cancer. In stage 4, the cancer has spread throughout the body. And patients with the diagnosis have a very low survival rate. The news was, of course, devastating to my family. My mom went through chemo and radiation over the next year, and everything was starting to look promising. She had fought hard, and the cancer had gone into remission.

Later in the year, I applied for the student manager job with the university's study abroad program and was offered the job in Prague. I accepted.

That summer, I headed off to Prague with my first group of students. I also did an internship in Ireland for a political party, Fianna Fáil. That summer cemented for me that I loved travel, and it planted the idea that maybe I could actually travel and work full time.

After my internship finished, I returned to the United States and found out my mom's cancer had returned. She tried more treatments over the next year or so, but nothing worked. She was eventually diagnosed as terminally ill, and there was nothing more the doctors could do. There was nothing left any of us could do, and it was crushing. After a two-year battle with cancer, my mother passed away on April 18, 2011. I was devastated.

Slowly, anger turned to grief, and very slowly, over the following years, I learned how to live with my loss. Travel was my coping mechanism.

My mother had always offered unconditional love and support, and I felt unmoored without her. It was time to start studying for my final exams, but my heart just wasn't in it. Part of me wanted to put off school and graduation until the next semester, but I knew my mom never would have wanted me to give up. So I buckled down, took all my exams, and somehow managed to pass my courses. I was cleared to graduate, but I still didn't know what I was going to do next.

I had a duty to fulfill that summer as a student manager, and I had a few weeks after graduating before I had to lead a group of forty students to Prague. I moved back home for a few weeks to see my family, mourn, and contemplate the next steps in life. Maybe I would take that feeling of having lost my anchor and use it as my reason to explore the world. Something inside me just felt, *Maybe this is the time.*

Admittedly, my main motivation for going overseas at that time was the fact that it was part of my obligations to the study abroad program, and it was paid for. But I already knew I wanted to transition into a more permanent way of working and traveling, so I got a one-way ticket instead of round-trip.

After the study abroad program finished in Prague, I landed a job teaching financial economics at the Czech University. Over the next year and a half, I worked and traveled to over thirty European countries. Working in the European Union (EU) as an American national came with a lot of restrictions and paperwork, which was how I learned that if I could find work in the EU, I could find work anywhere.

But I still didn't know just how permanent, or how fulfilling, my work and travel lifestyle could be. When my job in Prague ended, I returned to the United States and got a job on the trading floor at Wells Fargo (a real corporate job). I had a three-month contract, which would allow me to make enough money to move to Australia. I still thought

I had to make a trade-off—work now at a job I didn't like so I could travel later. I thought of my corporate job as a necessary evil. I didn't have a problem with it, since it was only a three-month contract, but now that I have a job I love, it seems odd to remember that I was once completely willing to trade the best hours of my day for something I hated.

After my Wells Fargo contract finished, I packed up my life and moved to Australia. I decided on Sydney, which is one of the most expensive cities in the world—especially for an American. At the time, Australian currency was worth quite a bit more than ours, so I knew I'd need to find a job right away. I put in six to eight hours every day job hunting, but I still made time for the beach (priorities!). Two and a half weeks later—job achieved. I was working at Quirqy, a tech startup, doing marketing and sales.

Australia was my first time "parachuting" into a brand-new country and getting set up immediately, with very little money saved and without having any prior knowledge about how things worked (other than how to get a visa). But what I learned from Australia was, *I can do this anywhere.* I can get a visa, move in, and get set up in a matter of weeks in a completely new country.

I stayed in Australia for six months, and then I was accepted, with a full scholarship, to the MBA program at the South Korean university. After studying in Korea for two years, I graduated and looked into finding work in marketing. I would have liked to stay and work in Korea, but there wasn't work in my field, especially as a foreign national. Earlier, when I wrote that working and traveling can put you in the right position to be able to move somewhere else for the right opportunity, Korea is where I learned that. Sometimes you can't always find the work you want where you are. So I headed off to New Zealand to try there.

To get a work visa in New Zealand, you only need $3,000 in your bank account, which was fortunate as I barely had that much. Once again, I landed and found work quickly. This time, it was remote marketing and sales work for a startup travel magazine. I had to be in New Zealand for this job, but even so, it was my first real remote job. That job was a major shift for me; it raised the bar for me in terms of the work I wanted to do. I learned that I could find remote jobs that paid well and allowed me total freedom over where I was and how I spent my time. The job was great, but the founders ran out of money and had to shut down the magazine. I spent four months working and two months traveling. While I was hitchhiking the South Island of New Zealand, my money started to dwindle. That was when I applied for my current job with Empire Flippers.

I landed the position as marketing and sales coordinator, and I moved to Southeast Asia, where I started my current role—a fully remote position that allows me to work and travel from wherever I want. I like to think of this as reaching "peak nomad."

Not quite a year later, I moved to Medellin, Colombia, where I now live. I currently spend around six to eight months in Colombia and the rest of the year traveling around the world.

You can create a stable home base and travel for part of the year like I do, or you can constantly be on the move to a new country every few months. Being a digital nomad means you have the freedom to live wherever you want and to move however often you want, while working a job you love.

CAPE VERDE

CENTRAL AFRICAN REPUBLIC   ☐

CHAPTER 2:

STUDYING ABROAD

My Experience Studying Abroad

In the previous chapter, I focused on how working and traveling can be a normal, sustainable way of life, something you can do for years. I also began to explain how working and traveling, done right, can help you progress toward your career goals.

In this chapter, we'll discuss one of the easiest ways to get started with the traveling lifestyle—studying abroad.

The study abroad program I completed was a fantastic experience, and it set me up perfectly for my transition into finding permanent work abroad. In my case, the focus of the program and courses were in international business, but I also received a practical education in traveling. You might even think of it as concurrent study; while you're taking your regular courses abroad, you're also taking International Travel 101—learning how to plan trips, navigate unfamiliar places, and research and prepare for a new culture.

Compared to backpacking, for example, studying abroad is structured and coordinated for you. It involves organizations you know and trust, like your university. Much of the paperwork and processes involved are simplified or just handled for you, and it comes with very clear goals and expectations. So it's probably one of the least stressful ways to explore travel for the first time.

I chose to study in Italy because, by that time, I had a few different connections to that country: I had been there myself on a trip with my father and brother, and a few of my good friends were also going to be in the program, so we would be able to travel together. After a bit of research, I found that I would be able to earn course credits toward my business degree, which was essential. Everything aligned to make it the perfect choice. To explain exactly what it looks like to do a study abroad program, below is a little bit about each of the places I went with my school's program.

BERGAMO, ITALY

This was my first extended trip and where I studied abroad. Bergamo is a small city of 115,000 people, about forty-five minutes outside of Milan. The city is surrounded by hills. And the heart of the city, the oldest part, is a historical center overlooking beautiful vistas. The city has expanded into the area around the hills, so there's like a modern ring of urban neighborhoods surrounding both the hills and the old city. From the outer modern area, you can take a funicular (it's like a cable car) into the old city, which feels very classical and European, with gorgeous old churches, city squares, narrow cobblestone streets—and all the buildings made of brick. There's also a lot of green space and trees, so nature's beauty is seen throughout the city as well. The pace of life, as you're walking around, feels slower and more relaxed than what you experience in most American cities. There are mouthwatering smells as you go from street to street—wine, beer, pasta, pizza. I would wander around during my free time, stopping for something to eat, always with gelato afterward—a new flavor every time. Everyone within earshot is speaking Italian, so you're surrounded by those relaxed cadences that make Italian such a beautiful language.

The students in the international business courses I took were about evenly divided between American and Italian, and our professors were from America, Italy, and other countries as well. The courses were extremely valuable, and I consider them to be some of the most rewarding school experiences I've ever had. We had plenty of free time between and after classes that we could spend exploring the city, and there were also tours and dinners organized for us to attend. The schedule even included a few four-day weekends, which we filled with trips to other parts of Europe. I found myself planning a lot of those trips and learning that I gravitated toward those planning activities, which helped point me in the direction of my next job. I applied to be a student manager in the program, and the next year I had my own group of students to prepare for Prague.

PRAGUE, CZECHIA

For this trip, I had been hired as the student manager, and it was my first year in that role. Though the actual trip was taken in the summer, we started work right away during the first semester of the school year, marketing the program and encouraging people to sign up. Immediately, I ran into a major problem. I found out the program needed to double its student enrollment from the previous year for Prague, or they would shut the trip down and no one would get to go. They'd had eight students the year before, and they needed at least fifteen. My senior leader and I were in charge of marketing for the course, so we needed to figure things out fast.

We started with a classic marketing strategy (networking) and expanded our efforts from there. Through my networking efforts, six to eight people I knew signed up, and we eventually had a total of thirty people sign up, making the program very popular.

For the next semester, my job was to teach the predeparture course. This meant I had to first learn all about Prague's history and culture so I could teach the group.

That summer was my first time seeing Prague, and I still think it's one of the most beautiful cities in the world. It has amazing traditional architecture, a huge castle, cathedrals, and old stone bridges over the river where you get the best views. It's absolutely stunning, and like a city from a fairy tale. Even seeing it, it's hard to believe it's real. There's a clock tower in the central "Old Town" area of the city, which houses Prague's astronomical clock. The clock itself is a medieval masterpiece that dates back to 1410, and as it strikes every hour (between 9 a.m. and 3 p.m.), twelve moving figurines designed to depict the apostles appear.

If you were to go there and walk around, you would definitely notice the smell of hops. Czechia has some of the best hops in the world, and some of the purest water, so they have the best ingredients for brewing beer. I learned that Czechia has the highest per capita beer consumption in the world, and the competition isn't even close. By far, Czechs drink the most beer in the world. They drink beer with every meal, sometimes even breakfast; the university has its own brewery; beer is actually cheaper than drinking water; it's a whole thing. The smell of hops is everywhere.

My first time in Prague was also my first year as a student manager. I was traveling with friends, just like I had in Italy, but this time I had to act as a manager in addition to being a friend. It was a balancing act, but it was also an experience that helped me grow as a person.

For my second year as a student manager, my duties for the first two semesters were the same (marketing the program and signing up students, and then teaching the predeparture course). My second summer was a little different, with my plan being to stay in Europe after the four-week study abroad program concluded—if I could find a job. Luckily, I landed a job teaching financial economics at the university in Prague. I was there for a year, and in addition to teaching financial economics, I even started a new IT course. While I was teaching, one of my mentors from the study abroad program introduced me to a professor from South Korea. We were both new to the country, so we got along really well. He knew from my previous mentor what I had done for my university's study abroad program by increasing their enrollment so dramatically, and that I had some accomplishments under my belt. I think he saw some potential in me, because he took me under his wing and started teaching me.

I moved on to Australia after a year at the university in Prague, and I kept in touch with that South Korean professor. A couple of years later, he suggested that I apply for a scholarship to study for my MBA in South Korea. I did, and I received a full scholarship.

GWANGJU, SOUTH KOREA

My scholarship covered all my tuition and my flights. For my living expenses, they helped me find work as a private English teacher. I also did a little office work at the university, helping edit English documents. I spent a year and a half in Korea, and for my last semester I went abroad to work on my thesis paper, which was about building a successful brand.

For me, the major learning experience in Korea was the cultural shift. I had already encountered European culture, which is different from American culture, but not as different as Korean culture. It was also my first time in Asia, so I was encountering this new culture for the first time.

Gwangju is a fairly large city of about 1.5 million people, and it happens to be the culinary capital of South Korea. Walking through the streets in the evening, you smell spicy food and hear loud music and see people dancing and partying, because Koreans love to go out in the evening and have dinner and drinks. Most of my classmates were Korean, and a little older, and they treated me like family—like their younger Korean brother. That really helped immerse me in the culture, because I had a whole community around me willing to teach me and show me about life in Korea. We got to know each other well and became very close.

Going for It

This book is about how to travel *and* make it work for your career goals. To accomplish that, you need to take stock of your educational trajectory—where you are, and where you're headed. What are you majoring in? What industry do you want to work in? What kinds of things do people in your industry do to find their first jobs or make themselves stand out? How could you arrange your travel experience so that it helps you accomplish those things?

In the case of studying abroad, you want to figure out how to do it in a manner that helps you complete your degree, exposes you to the country or industry where you want to work, expands your network, or even helps you get work experience. Choosing a study abroad trip just because the country where you're going is beautiful, or a major tourist destination, or has good nightclubs isn't going to help you reach your long-term goals. You need to be a little more focused on exactly how the trip will benefit you professionally.

To use myself as an example (surprise!), I wanted to study abroad so I could see Italy again, but I also saw very specific benefits to enrolling in the program: it would help me complete my business degree, and it would expose me to different styles of teaching business, since we would learn from American, Italian, and other international professors. Once I realized that there was a job opportunity with the program itself, I knew I could also get work experience while covering most of my travel expenses, which was an amazing bonus.

Here are some important factors to consider as you look at different study abroad programs:

- Timing

  First, consider that a study abroad program tends to make the most sense if you're a sophomore or junior. If you're a freshman, they may not even let you go, but that's okay. That's the best time to begin your research so you can line up your courses in the most logical and expedient way and start to plan out the finances. If you can decide exactly what course you'll take with the study abroad program, you can get started obtaining any prerequisite credits you'll need. You can also start saving up and planning your finances for the trip. You can start preparing almost as soon as you enroll as a freshman.

  But that's not to say you've missed your chance if you're a senior, or even if you've already graduated. You can always continue your education. Work on earning an MBA, a master's, or a PhD. Especially in America, we tend to think of education as something you do when you're young. You take classes, get your degree, and never go back. But more and more, people are going back to school as established adults, to switch careers or gain a new skill or credential. So a study abroad program is still something you can consider, and there are still opportunities to do it for free, like with my full scholarship to study in South Korea.

If you are out of school and want to enroll in a study abroad program, start by looking up the school you graduated from (if you have a degree). Take a look at their master's programs, for example, see what they offer that can be done abroad, and then start looking into scholarships.

You can also start by looking at schools that you would like to attend overseas. To make sure they're accredited and internationally recognized, look to see if they're affiliated with any American professional organizations. For example, international business schools are accredited by the Association to Advance Collegiate Schools of Business (AACSB). If you're interested in an MBA, you can look up the AACSB list of accredited schools, which are all over the world (including America—Harvard is AACSB accredited). This is a key step to making sure your international degree will be recognized by American employers.

At the same time, you can start figuring out the finances. Look around for private scholarships, which will sometimes give you money that just has to go toward your education (rather than a specific program), start setting aside some of your income for a travel fund, and look into tax benefits for education savings accounts. In Missouri, we have a program called MOST, which is a savings account you can use to save up for any kind of education and receive different tax benefits on the money you put into that account.

- How to Find Opportunities to Study Abroad

  If you're in a business school or program, most business schools have a study abroad program; this will be the easiest way for you to get started.

  If you are in a different program, such as engineering, one strategy is to add a business minor to your degree so you can access the study abroad program. This is not just about "gaming the system" so you can go overseas, either—a business minor can make sense for many different disciplines. In engineering, for example, lots of engineers work as consultants, which means they run their own business.

  If you are not in a business program, and adding a business minor is not a good option for you, then start investigating your university's international center. Most major universities have one. This center provides other programs and options for international study.

  Failing both of these options, there are third-party companies that coordinate study abroad programs— like CIEE, which is one of the largest nonprofit organizations that promotes international exchange and study abroad programs. This option requires more effort on your part; you'll need to research the companies you're considering to make sure they're reputable, ask around to make sure that any credit you earn through the third party will be accepted by your school, and get a detailed breakdown of what is covered in the cost of the program so you can figure out if it makes sense for you. Compare their cost with what you would pay to take a course through your university. You need to consider the room and board costs in addition to tuition to make sure it's a worthwhile investment.

- Benefits You Can Put on Your Resume (or CV, or Course Transcript)

A good program, as I've said, should give you more than just the chance to see another part of the world; it should help you finish your program or get the kind of work experience you're looking for. Look for programs that offer the courses you need toward your degree, and consult with a student advisor to make sure the credit offered will work for your degree requirements.

Alternatively, depending on your degree, you might want exposure to a particular country or language. Say you're working toward a degree in translation and specializing in Spanish. Traveling to a Spanish-speaking country will already be a must, and the more traveling you can do, the better. If you're studying international law, a trip to the Netherlands would allow you to visit the Hague, where the International Court of Justice is located. The idea here is to consider what countries or cities might be relevant to your specific discipline and career goals. Again, consulting with a student advisor is a great way to figure this out. Another great option is to add on an international internship, which we will go over later.

- Work and Travel Balance

  The program I completed was structured into four weeks, with two four-day weekends scheduled so students could go traveling around the region. That's important because it allows you to reap the full benefits of being in another country: interacting with new people, learning the language, getting immersed in another culture. So be wary of travel opportunities that are purely work or that are highly structured with little free time. If you're paying to travel somewhere, you should make sure you'll have time to enjoy it, see everything, and gain all the experience possible.

- Logistics (Accommodations, Food, Transportation)

  For a study abroad program, I think it's best for as much of this stuff to be handled through the university as possible. If you have a choice between handling things yourself or going with whatever the university has set up, I suggest taking the university option. This leaves you free to focus on your studies and traveling in your time off. Take full advantage of any events, tours, or dinners that are planned or sponsored for you while you're abroad, if only on principle. There will be free food and all the costs were included in your fees, so you've already paid for it. You might as well enjoy it!

- Preparation

  A good study abroad course should offer some fairly comprehensive preparation for going overseas. They should tell you what the culture is like, what the courses you'll be taking will be like, what kinds of things you can and can't do, important rules and regulations, and maybe even some basic language lessons. They may also offer basic traveling tips, including what to pack and how to book a flight. My program offered a course that was one hour a week for half a semester. We covered all the above and more, including culture-specific body language and gestures. Italians use body language a lot, so there are gestures you need to learn to avoid so you don't offend anyone. You don't need to be an expert, but being familiar with the country you plan to study or travel in is always a good idea.

  Preparation is key. It will help you get the most out of your experience. And since you usually take these courses with the other students you'll be traveling with, it's also a great way to get acquainted.

  If the program doesn't offer a preparation course or opportunity, you can compensate with your own research—guidebooks, YouTube, apps. There are so many ways to get the information ahead of time.

- Friends (a.k.a. Support System)

  The best way to take part in a study abroad program, in my opinion, is with a group of people you know. Even though I had other reasons for wanting to go to Italy, part of the reason I chose that location was because I had a few friends who were also going. If you don't already have friends who are planning to go, you can always make some along the way. The main thing is to be open about building new connections and creating a community for yourself and others, even if it takes you a little outside your comfort zone. Everyone needs a support system sometimes, especially when you're away from home. Also, practically speaking, a lot of the activities you'll be doing will be in groups, so it's a good idea to get to know people and figure out who you enjoy spending time with—and those you don't (hopefully, there won't be many among your travel companions).

- Cost

  When evaluating the cost of a program, compare it to the tuition you would pay to take a class at home. Consider that when you pay tuition for a course at home, you're still paying living expenses as well, so factor that in too. If it works out to roughly the same whether you're at home or abroad (not including airfare, which is always an additional expense), that means you're getting a great deal—paying the same as you'd pay to take a class at home but in another country, as a completely new experience and with tons of chances to do more traveling while you're there. If the study abroad program is more expensive but covers things like airfare, food, or accommodations, then it could still be a good fit. The airfare is the major cost since it's generally not included. Regarding living expenses, Americans tend to have the perception that Europe is expensive, but it's not always the case. Prague was actually cheaper, in terms of living expenses, than most large American cities.

Also ask around for ways to lower costs. Often, if you work for the program, you can get free travel. Find out when they'll be hiring—it's generally once a year. You have nothing to lose by applying! In my case, as a student manager I received paid airfare, housing, and a food stipend. Another option to ask about is travel scholarships, either through the program, faculty, or a third party.

Facing Challenges

Studying abroad does come with its own set of challenges, but they're not as scary or as insurmountable as you might think. Often when people are considering studying abroad, they just have vague unnamed fears about what could go wrong. When you actually name the challenges and think clearly about them, you can see there's a way to handle everything.

- Language

  Depending on your exposure to the language and your aptitude, you may find it a little easier or harder to pick up new languages. Some people find it easier to write in a new language than to speak it, or vice versa, but bottom line, you're going to need to learn how to communicate in international settings. One fact that may put your mind a bit more at ease is that in many countries, many of the younger people can speak some level of English. That does not, however, mean you shouldn't know some of their language as well. You don't have to be perfectly fluent, just "functional." The good news is, there are tons of resources out there to help you learn—from software and audio courses to YouTube videos and Google Translate. And once you're immersed in a new country, you'll learn the language a lot faster than you would if you were at home. Still, it helps to study the language in advance and learn the basics before you arrive.

Being an Ambassador

When you study abroad, everywhere you go, you're an ambassador for the university. As an American, you're an ambassador for American culture, and it's up to you whether you're going to enforce the negative stereotypes people may have or leave a positive impression. Many times, when you come into contact with someone, you may be the first American they've ever met, so it's a big responsibility.

• Community

Bring one, or make your own, but you're going to need people around you who you can talk to and hang out with. If you're traveling with friends, that makes things a lot easier. However, if you travel long enough, there will be times when you'll be on your own and will need to improvise.

People may try to avoid being alone by basing travel decisions around family and friends, but you will eventually want to go somewhere where your family or group of friends doesn't, and then you'll have a choice to make. Personally, I don't think you can travel effectively if you're always surrounded by a comfortable group. If traveling is about furthering your goals, how can you do that if you're always compromising between your goals and everyone else's? I've traveled alone for extended periods of time, all over the world, and it was sometimes difficult. But they were also some of the most valuable and rewarding learning experiences I have ever had.

When you travel by yourself, even the most extro-verted person will get lonely after a while. You realize how important those social connections really are when you don't have them anymore, and you find yourself surrounded by acquaintances or semi-friends—people you're friendly with but don't know very well yet. In that situation, you have to learn how to make yourself approachable and how to become comfortable approaching others. It can take some work, but it is also a huge opportunity for personal growth, because no one is really com-fortable just walking up to strangers and starting a conversation. Not at first. It's something you have to learn over time.

• Everyday Challenges

Another challenge may come from the frustration of trying to complete some kind of task that's easy for you at home but that is done quite differently in another country. For example, one worldly struggle is trying to do laundry in a strange city. At home, you might have a washer and dryer in your house. Doing laundry in a foreign country can vary drastically—in some places they will wash, dry, and fold your laun-dry for a reasonable amount, but some cities just don't have this service available. In Western Europe, laundromats are typically easy to find, but in Eastern Europe, they are few and far between in some areas and can cost US$10 to $15 to wash and dry one load.

If you're studying abroad, figuring out how to take care of this particular task won't be difficult. You'll have people and resources to help you out. If you're traveling on your own, it can be a serious challenge. Doing some research before you travel is always a good idea. But if you decide to go somewhere on the spur of the moment, you might not have time to figure it out beforehand. In that case, ask the staff at wherever you decide to stay. Just remember that patience is crucial to traveling successfully. Things *will* be different in another country. Just take a breath, use your head, and figure it out. You can do it!

A note about medical systems abroad: A lot of Americans worry about health care. We tend to be skeptical of other countries' health care systems, yet I think this concern is mostly unfounded. There are excellent hospitals in all the countries I've been to. Colombia actually has about twenty-two of the top forty-three hospitals in Latin America. Both Thailand and Colombia are well-known medical tourism destinations. In these countries, you can get routine or complicated procedures done, in state-of-the-art facilities, by English-speaking doctors, for a fraction of the cost you would pay at home.

So those are some of the challenges you'll face when studying abroad. But as I've said, there are also tons of benefits. In addition to helping your resume or CV, there is also the intangible knowledge you'll gain. When I went to Italy, I quickly fell into the role of travel planner; we were going on all these day trips and weekend trips, and I found myself doing a lot of the coordinating for where we would go and where we would stay. I realized I loved it. That was part of what drew me to apply to the student manager program later on and, in a way, helped to set me on the course that I've been on ever since.

You never know what you'll learn about yourself when you travel, but it's something that's worth being mindful about as you go. Take notice of which new activities you enjoy the most, what roles you seem to fill when you're in a group, what skills you use to handle an unexpected situation. That part of it, of immersing yourself into an unfamiliar setting and seeing what happens, is what makes people discover things they are passionate about. You gain a sense of clarity about who you are, what you're good at, and what you want out of life.

Another Study Abroad Option –
Semester at Sea

This is an option to study for a semester on a cruise ship and travel internationally. Semester at Sea is accredited through Colorado State University.

Benefits, Both Professional and Personal

In this book, I put a lot of emphasis on the ways travel can further your career ambitions, because I think that's something a lot of people don't think of when they think of traveling. But that's not to say there aren't huge personal benefits, too.

Probably one of the most lasting benefits I've come away with is the confidence that I can successfully do something that's unfamiliar or that I'm not too sure about. I'm less fearful of the risks involved in the opportunities I want to take, because I know I can handle whatever happens. That has really empowered me to keep taking chances on new opportunities and keep progressing down the path that I chose, toward living and working abroad. And the vague fears that I used to have about travel? They've all turned out to be pointless, which was another useful lesson.

Another sort of "big-picture" benefit was learning about other cultures and seeing that there's more than one kind of society and more than one way to live.

Studying in Europe gave me exposure to other educational systems. I was impressed by how well-educated people were outside of America, and how many different educational systems there are—some of which are much better than those in America. Many European countries offer free university, including the university in Prague, so no one is prevented from getting a degree because of money. I like the idea that education is available to all who want to pursue it, regardless of their financial status.

Getting that immersive exposure to other cultures, at a time in my life when I hadn't experienced it before, really opened my eyes to other ways of living and seeing the world. For instance, in the United States, it's very common to see people making work their top priority, and sacrificing their home and social lives for that. In contrast, what I saw in Europe was people putting family, friends, travel, and experiences before work. People treated work as something that funds the life they want to have, rather than what we sometimes do in America, which is trying to make work something all-encompassing, that takes all our time and energy and meets all or most of our emotional needs.

Every year, new studies and articles show that Americans receive the least paid vacation time from their employers than workers in other developed countries—and that most Americans don't use the little bit of vacation time their employers allow. So when you go abroad as an American, one of the first things you notice is that work holds a different place in people's lives. They work hard at their jobs, but it's something they regard as a "part" of their lives, one small part of what makes them happy and what gives them a sense of purpose. That was really inspiring to me, and it got me thinking about some of principles I had never questioned before. In America, being a workaholic seems normal, and sometimes even expected. Even ordinary jobs can come with the expectation that employees will voluntarily sacrifice other things for them. I found it interesting to look at all those accepted values in a new light, which I did because I was in a country where people have a different approach to life. I found that I much prefer the way Europeans approach work and the place it has in their lives. Finding the perfect work-to-life balance is something that takes time, and every country has their own approach!

Other than work, I started to learn what it meant to be an American, in a global sense, once I started traveling. People will figure out that you're American, and it will affect how they interact with you. This can be a new experience for people (it was for me) if you've never traveled outside the United States and seen your culture from the outside—how people interact with you, what questions they ask, what assumptions they make. American culture is so effectively exported and packaged through Hollywood and pop culture that people do have an idea of what American culture is, and they even know quite a bit about our politics. So another benefit to traveling is learning to see your own cultural identity a little more objectively.

I learned that in Eastern Europe, Americans are known for smiling a lot. It's considered a weird behavior of ours. Facial expressions are a lot more neutral in some parts of the world, so Americans can seem a little over the top with all our smiling and emoting. As a traveler, you have to adjust to the culture you're visiting and interpret other people's body language correctly so you don't take offense or think someone is upset when they're actually not.

Americans also tend to live a lot more independently than other cultures. For better or worse, we're very individualistic. In Italy, it's common for men to live with their parents and siblings until they're married. It's a standard way to live. For most Americans, we live at home until eighteen or so, and then go to college and start this transitional period where we sort of live on our own in a dorm or with roommates, not really making our own money (or at least not much of it), and not really "adulting" in our sense of the word, cooking and cleaning and completely taking care of ourselves. And then in our twenties, we move toward full independence, living on our own and making our own money. (For those who don't go to college, the timing is often still similar, only it typically includes continuing to live with parents instead of in a dorm.) At least, that tends to be the goal, even if it doesn't always happen.

But in some other countries, they don't have that same quick transition to independence as an adult. They don't move out until they get married; they're much more collectivistic, in the sense of being very comfortable living and operating as a family or in groups. When you travel, you'll notice that you see groups of people from England or Australia. When you see someone on their own, there's a good chance they're American. It's interesting to see the places where your own culture kind of diverges from what you realize is the more common trend.

I mentioned earlier how traveling abroad is a good addition to your resume. To expand on that, when you graduate and start interviewing for jobs, one of your main objectives is to have something to talk about to show your work experience. And because most people don't have much conventional work experience at this point, you have to get creative. Studying abroad is something that can help fill that gap, and the way to do that effectively is to make sure, while you're studying abroad, that you are creating some talking points about things you did on the trip.

For me, it was planning the weekend trips, and then it was finding my job as a professor. Something that came out of the study abroad program, but kind of pushed it a little further: "I went on a study abroad program, and then I started doing a lot of travel coordinating with my friends." You want to have something to show that you got a little extra experience out of it.

Coming Back Home

"Coming back" might sound a little obvious. Everyone knows how to come back home. But I'm talking about how you process and celebrate your travel experience, and things to consider as you settle back into your life.

While you're traveling, keep an eye out for souvenirs—and I mean this in a broad sense. A souvenir can be something like a photo. I love landscape photography, so the photos I take are one of the main ways that I celebrate the places I've been. Some travelers are collectors. I know people who collect currency from different places, or jars of sand from every beach they've been to. Then there are your memories—new foods you tried, crazy experiences you had, or things you learned. Those are all souvenirs. When you're back home, they'll help remind you of your experience and become a way to solidify those memories.

You also have to figure out your approach to talking about your travels. Personally, I try to be a little sensitive when talking about my adventures. You can experience so much on a trip that when you come home and try to tell your friends and family about it, you kind of wear out their attention span. We actually covered this in the predeparture courses that I taught—it's called the honeymoon stage. You go abroad, fall in love with a country, and when you come back, you're still in that honeymoon stage and want to talk about it to everyone. But just because someone asks you how your trip was, that doesn't mean they want you to talk about Venice for hours straight. So you learn to gauge people's interest, and then give them the short version. If they seem really interested, or it turns out they've also been to that country, or something like that, then you can expand. It's tough to restrain yourself when you're talking about something that's so amazing. But the truth is, you'll never be able to fully tell someone else what it was like. They have to go for themselves.

You also have to learn how to read the room a little bit. If you're coming back from a study abroad program, you might be talking to someone who just spent the summer working a minimum wage job. That would definitely be an example of a time when you might give the "short version" of your travel story, and then move on to a different subject.

It can feel odd returning to your home country after living abroad. This is still part of the experience—noticing what feels strange and if you're seeing things differently. This will influence the ways that your trip changes your life in a more permanent way.

I think it's important to note, here at the end of this chapter, that this point—when you've come home and it might feel a little weird—can be one of the points where you realize that you want to make different choices for your life. For example, I had noticed all those things about American work/life culture, when I was abroad and got to see it from the outside, that would lead to me choosing what I think is a more balanced approach. Over the following years, I created a life where my personal pursuits, like travel, are given much more space than they had when I lived in the United States.

This is why it's important to know that it's possible to work and live abroad as long as you want. So that at a point like this, when you realize that your study abroad program showed you a way of life that you actually like and want for yourself, you'll know that you can really make it happen.

In the next chapter, I'll discuss interning abroad, which can be one type of experience that can give you a better idea of what it's like to work and live abroad before you jump into the deep end.

GERMANY   ☐

CHAPTER 3:

INTERNING ABROAD

When most people think of an internship, they think of a large company, uninspiring work, maybe interning at the company where their mom or dad works. People don't necessarily think of doing an internship overseas. Much like the whole idea of traveling and working abroad, it can seem impractical to Americans.

But internships can be meaningful, with real responsibilities, and when you combine it with traveling overseas, it becomes a much broader and more immersive learning experience. Like studying abroad, you get more value out of it; not only learning your way around an office job for maybe the first time, but also learning your way around a culture.

Compared to studying abroad, interning overseas is sort of the next difficulty level (to use a gaming metaphor). As an international student, you're enveloped in a structured environment that's designed to minimize your confusion and help you function. As an intern, that safety net is gone. You receive training for your job, but there are no more tours or dinners arranged for you, no guidebooks, no predeparture course. It's freeing and challenging, and it can be a little bit scary, but in a good way. When you come out the other side, with a new set of office anecdotes and one or two solid work references, it'll be a great accomplishment.

Internships are becoming a widespread requirement in the job market. Many university programs are structured to include an internship, and it's something that can give you a leg up in the job market, if done right.

Although, not all internships are created equally. The value of the internship depends on where you're working, the tasks you're doing, what kind of experience you're gaining. An internship at your dad's company is not as interesting as having worked for a Fortune 500 company, and that's not as interesting as having worked in a different country.

After I finished my MBA in Gwangju, I was living in South Korea and looking for work in my discipline, and I took a job for a company that helps people find internships in another country for a fee. It's only in America that an overseas internship might seem like an odd thing to do. In other countries, it's much more common, because it's such an effective way to get started in the job market. The value of interning in another country is that it dramatically expands your network. If you've been working and studying in your home state in the United States, your network is basically within that state—maybe with a few out-of-state contacts. But as soon as you work outside the country, your network expands to include international contacts. So this is a great way to set a strong foundation for your career—and it's particularly good for someone who is looking to live and work abroad for an extended period. Those contacts will be very helpful for finding work or resources as you travel.

My Experience as an Intern

The work that I did as a student manager for the study abroad program with my university was technically an internship. That was my first intern experience. I found the Prague program to be a challenge, but it was extremely rewarding when I was able to succeed with that challenge.

After that success, the director of the study abroad program took an interest in me—he actually became one of my mentors. He reached out to his contacts to see if he could find me an internship in another country. He found me an amazing opportunity as an intern for Fianna Fáil, a Republican Irish political party. I had a supervisor, but my ultimate boss was the General Secretary of Ireland, and I was helping with voter outreach on Irish university campuses, trying to get the youth vote. The internship was one month, based in Dublin, and I was there for two months. I even had help with housing since the study abroad program had a location there.

You may be reading this thinking, "Well, great, this guy got lucky and found an awesome opportunity. How am I going to do that?" Yes, I was fortunate—but at the same time, a lot of hard work went into getting myself to a position where I knew people who were willing and able to help me. The fact that I had a mentor wasn't an accident. I worked really hard to build up the Prague program, and I was also open and looking for a mentor. So when the director took an interest in me, I was ready for that opportunity. When he started asking around to help me find an internship, he was able to give me a genuine, good recommendation because he had seen my work. This is all part of networking.

Networking is a hugely important part of living and traveling abroad, and it's something I highly recommend, but I want to be clear on what I mean by networking. It's not just about finding people who are useful to you and being nice to them. A good network is founded on genuine connections. Good contacts are people you know, people you've spent time with or have stuff in common with, people whose work is in some way relevant to yours.

To build your network, you put yourself in situations like the lunch break at work, like happy hour, places where you'll be around people you're already somehow connected with. Then you strengthen those connections by genuinely taking an interest in others, finding common ground with them, and sharing about yourself with them, including your work background and career goals. It's about putting yourself out there, because telling people what you want is still a kind of vulnerability, and being open to whatever suggestions or assistance might come out of it. At the same time, you're also genuinely listening to others, offering any advice or help that you can, and—above all—relaxing and being yourself. Later in this chapter, I'll explain office networking and how to spot the right opportunities to mingle.

Ireland in 2009 and 2010 was a politically fraught situation. Since I was working on a campaign, I became immersed in the politics over there. It was a tense time; the economic crisis was starting to hit Europe in significant ways after the 2008 housing crash in the United States. Fianna Fáil had been the governing party for eight to nine years, so they were taking much of the blame for the economic struggles the Irish people were experiencing.

While I was there, when I was introduced to new people,

I actually stopped telling them what my job was, because I found people were very passionate about the political situation over there, and it wasn't always a good way to start a conversation. But overall, it was a great experience. Everyone I met was friendly, and, of course, the learning experience from a situation like that was extremely valuable. My internship involved a lot of business-related tasks and responsibilities, and this was where I really committed to doing international business. It clicked that this industry was where I wanted to be.

My previous travel experience was with the study abroad program, so I was used to doing things with large groups. We traveled a lot as a group, so there were always friends with me and people from America, and the program was designed for people who were unfamiliar with the country. In contrast, as an intern, I was the only American in the entire office, and the training wheels were off. The expectation was that I would keep up with everyone else.

This was also my first time in an office setting, and there was a lot more responsibility and much higher expectations, even as I was trying to get up to speed on the culture and even the language. Unsurprisingly, Irish English is officially considered its own dialect (with tons of local variants), and it's very different from American English. A lot of my job was calling universities, and I had to try to quickly get comfortable with Irish accents and slang so that I could communicate effectively.

With the study abroad program, I had seen the value of preparing and researching before going into a new country. I did this as best as I could, but particularly working in politics, much of it you have to learn on the ground from talking to people.

GUINEA

What really helped was the people I worked with. Many of them were political science graduates, just like you would see working on a political campaign in America. Their education had covered American politics in detail, not to mention Irish politics, which they knew extremely well, so it wasn't easy to measure up. But it meant they were able to talk me through the issues of the campaign and help me understand Irish politics. They were welcoming and nice, and a lot of the tasks they gave me were things that I could do without being an expert on Irish politics. There was also a good age range in the office, anywhere from early twenties to fifties, so I was able to build connections and get to know people outside the office.

As I mentioned in the previous chapter, it's important to have a community of some kind when you're traveling and working, and here it was easy to build one for myself, so that was a big plus. Work friends are very important when you're abroad because those contacts are personal *and* professional, so you're building your professional network at the same time as creating friendships. I'm still in touch with a lot of the people I met there.

When I think of my time in Ireland now, I mostly remember the friendly people and the work/life balance they enjoyed. As I mentioned in the previous chapter, I found that Europeans have a different take on how to prioritize work with the rest of their life, and I really appreciated that.

I can also clearly remember the lush green countryside, and a lot of their monuments and statues are greenish as well, so that's definitely a color that I associate with Ireland now. I remember Irish fish and chips extremely fondly—it was one of my favorite dishes over there, and not the same as American fish and chips at all. It was also something you could smell as you were walking by, when a restaurant was preparing it, so then I'd have to go in and order some. I did have to adjust some of my expectations. I had assumed everyone would drink Guinness, but it turns out the young people actually prefer Budweiser because it doesn't fill you up as much. I certainly had not expected to see so many people drinking American-style beer in Ireland.

One of my favorite memories is from when I returned to Ireland after having been gone about two years. I met up with one of my Irish friends and he showed me around. I was there for St. Patrick's Day, so it was amazing to be in Dublin with some Irish friends to show me around all the places and celebrations. My friend was on his way to becoming a politician; he had a law degree, and he had worked for Senator John McCain in the United States, so it was like our experiences were sort of mirrored. It was great to be able to call him up after a couple of years and hang out in Dublin. That's one of my favorite outcomes of networking. It's not always about finding a job or getting a favor. It's just as much about having people you've connected with, who you can spend time with.

Opportunities

Odd as it may sound, one of the opportunities to keep an eye out for when you're interning is lunchtime. Think about it—it's one of the few chances to socialize, and it's when you can really build your connections with people. You just have to put yourself out there a little bit, and just ask around, "Hey, is anyone going to get lunch?" Especially if it's an unpaid internship, you may be tempted to regularly take your lunch to work and eat at your desk. And if you're not naturally social, you might plan to go straight home at the end of the day. But if you do that, you're not making yourself accessible at all. You'll never really get to know anyone, and your network won't grow. You're interning to make connections. This is your chance. Going out with coworkers is an important investment in your network.

Part of the reason I would recommend focusing on networking when you're doing an internship, rather than simply putting your nose to the grindstone, is because the chances you'll actually end up working for that company are probably slim, unless that's something you've set out to accomplish. There are two kinds of internship opportunities—the ones that can lead to permanent work, and the ones where you're just interested in the job experience. Unless you're planning to relocate to that country, or you're graduating in a few years (like I was), chances are that an international internship is primarily about the job experience.

Even so, it's crucial to be as great at your job as you can be, and to try to overachieve where possible. It's about making a good impression on the people around you so you can build your network and get work references. So your tasks are an opportunity to introduce yourself to people, in a way—to show them who you are as a person and employee.

Benefits

As I've mentioned, internships are more immersive than study abroad programs; it's sort of like getting thrown into the deep end of the local culture instead of wading through the shallow end. You also tend to pick up work skills and knowledge in addition to learning about the culture. Chances are, this will be one of your first jobs in an office, so it will be your introduction to the office environment, where you'll learn the general skills needed for that environment, such as how to get along with others, how to avoid stepping on toes, and how to make yourself useful.

Typically, international internships are not paid—that would necessitate tons of paperwork to get a work visa, which is usually not worth it for a two-to-three-month internship. Instead, it's not uncommon for the company to offer to cover housing or some meals. For you as an intern, the benefits of the internship are more intangible. It's about getting good business experience and building a network.

A good internship should also be a bridge to your next career goal. Just like the study abroad program, you want it to help you get somewhere. But in the case of an internship, you should be thinking beyond, "I can put this on my resume." You want to make sure this internship offers you something specific to your goals. For instance, through my work with the study abroad program, I learned that I wanted to get into international business. For that, you need international work experience, and the internship in Ireland was my way of getting that. Your internship should be relevant to the kind of work or industry you want to be involved with.

If you are looking for internships that can turn into permanent work, make sure to look for opportunities that clearly state this is a possibility. Even if it's not clearly stated, that's something you can ask about in the interview process: "Is there any opportunity after I finish my internship to apply for a full-time role?" This can also be something to mention to your boss or manager when you start the opportunity—that you would be open to joining the organization full time and would like to know how to help that happen. It's important to be upfront about what you want out of the opportunity, because that will change the way your boss and coworkers see you. A lot of times, the intern role is pretty flexible and amorphous; it comes with a list of tasks and responsibilities, but they're not set in stone. You should have a lot of power to expand that role and make it meaningful, just by being clear on what you're hoping to gain and asking for more tasks or responsibilities if you feel you can handle them.

Even if the internship doesn't become a permanent job, you have it on your resume and you can leverage that for all it's worth. List the tasks you performed, as well as any specific achievements or completed projects, and mention any soft skills or communication skills you developed. You can use examples from your internship in interviews—it's always best to offer real-life examples. You can dedicate a paragraph to it on your cover letter, which should, of course, be customized for the specific company and role you're applying to.

Another benefit of an internship is that you will learn how a company works without working for that same company for years. It's less common now, but there are still people in professions like engineering or law who graduate, get hired at a company, and stay there for decades. When you work for just one company right out of school, you're completely formed by that company. All your expectations for how things should work, your habits and instincts, they're all specific to that one office.

By contrast, an internship allows you to get a good look at how a particular company does business, but you're not committed to them. Then, when you graduate and get a "career job," you've already had some exposure to other approaches. You're already a little more informed and a little more flexible. I think it's good to work a lot of different jobs, in different industries, in different countries. That strengthens you as a person and as an employee, making you more well-rounded and resilient.

International Internships Broaden Your Future's Horizons

Any internship should help you start to learn how a company works, but an international internship is even more beneficial—because you're also learning how another *country* works at the same time. And that can really broaden your mind and expose you to so many different ways of living and working. You also gain international friends and references, making it easier for you to find work in other parts of the world if you later decide that's what you want to do.

When you do an international internship, it's a lot more obvious to your boss and coworkers that you're serious about the opportunity and about advancing your career, or you wouldn't have traveled all that way. It shows that you're highly motivated. That kind of paves the way for things like work references. The people you ask for a reference need to feel confident that they know you and can recommend your work. And when people know that you're from another country, that's something memorable and impressive that helps you make a good impression from the beginning.

Over the course of the internship, you can start setting the stage to ask for a reference from someone who knows you and your work. My work references were extremely helpful for me—I already had the director of the study abroad program as a reference, and my intern boss became another reference, as well as a professor I worked closely with on the study abroad program. Those all came about as a result of networking; I had built those relationships, and done enough work that impressed those particular people, that it was appropriate to get references from them.

As I mentioned, internships are becoming the norm in business schools—mine made it a requirement the year after I graduated. And they're becoming the norm in almost every discipline. So even if your program doesn't require an internship, it's a smart idea to do one, because chances are your competition in the job market will have internships on their resumes, even if you don't.

An international internship gives you a competitive edge. Even if all the other job candidates have an internship, you'll be one of the few who went overseas for it. It tends to prove that this was a "real" internship, not a summer working at your mom or dad's company. You've gained more value from the experience since it was in another country and there was so much more to learn, so it becomes a talking point in interviews and something that recruiters will notice just from looking at your resume, even before they interview you.

Apprenticeships

Apprenticeships are much more structured than internships. They're usually paid, but they are training programs, so the pay will be less than what you will earn when you finish the apprenticeship. There is usually the stated intention that you will join the business after a learning period of six months or whatever it is. So if you're graduating or have graduated and are looking for opportunities that will turn into permanent work, apprenticeships are a good option.

Finding and Preparing for an International Internship

Essentially, an international internship is a way to do something that's becoming almost a standard requirement, in a way that stands out. You'll still need to be selective about the kind of internship you do—make sure it's a role that will actually be meaningful and will help move you toward your future goals. Even though the overall theme in this book is that you can travel *and* live abroad *and* make good money with a career that you really want, this particular option—interning—is not about making money right away; even an amazing internship might be unpaid. This is an option where you invest now to reap the rewards later.

To begin your internship on a strong note, arrive in the country well in advance—maybe a week, or even two. This will give you time to settle in and learn your way around. Early on, identify people you might want to use as reference later. The best candidates are bosses or managers with direct supervision of your work. But network as broadly as possible, because you never know who you'll run into later.

Some of the most valuable skills you can gain from an international internship are soft skills. Adapting to a new culture and office environment can make you more flexible and approachable, which can help you stand out in an interview. Ultimately, people hire people they want to work with, not just those who have the skills they want on paper. Traveling naturally helps develop your soft skills—learning to put yourself out there, build connections with new people, and be approachable. These are all things you have to do when you're in a new country. And they're extremely valuable skills in today's job market, where employers are starting to emphasize interpersonal and communication skills.

To find an internship, the same process applies that I outlined in the previous chapter. Start with your university and exhaust all the resources they have to offer—through your faculty, student advisor, or any internship placement programs the school may run. If you don't have an international network of your own, ask your friends and family, as well as any professors you may have gotten to know. Large companies like the "big four" in accounting, or companies like IBM, Accenture, etc., may have offices all over the world, so if you know someone in America who works for a large multinational, they may know about international internship opportunities. Getting an internship tends to be about who you know, so make sure to ask around. Someone you know may be able to arrange the perfect opportunity.

There are also third-party options, similar to the company I worked for in South Korea. The biggest one is called CIEE.org, and they are the leading nonprofit NGO in international education. They help coordinate international education and exchange, and they also have their own internships. Most third-party options will charge a fee, so don't be put off if you run into that; there's nothing wrong with paying for an internship as long as you get a valuable experience out of it.

Factors to consider when looking at internships:

- Goal

  If you're about to graduate, you might be more interested in internships or apprenticeships that could lead to permanent work. If you're going back to school in the fall or the following semester, you probably just want the experience. Figure this out first, because it will affect the kinds of opportunities you apply for.

- Length

  In my opinion, you need at least two months to get true value from an internship experience. The first week or so is just getting up to speed, so to get any real tasks accomplished, at least a month is necessary.

- Tasks and Responsibilities

  The job tasks are usually listed when you apply for the internship. You will want to take a close look at the language that's used to try to make sure it will be a meaningful role for you. You'll also want to ask follow-up questions if you get the chance to try to clarify exactly what you'll be doing. Look for responsibilities that align with the skills you're looking to build. Will you get a chance to work with specific software or technology? Will you be in a department that is related to your interests? Maybe the tasks will be a mix of things you're interested in or familiar with and some things that will be totally new. That can certainly be worthwhile, as getting out of your comfort zone is always a good learning experience.

•   Housing and Arrangements

    Depending on how you find the internship, you may or may not receive assistance with finding housing. If you go with a third-party company and pay a fee, you should reasonably expect some assistance. If you find the internship yourself or through a personal connection, there might not be that supportive infrastructure.

It's also important to have your paperwork in order. If you're doing an international internship, you'll most likely be on a tourist visa. So when you pass through customs, you have to be very clear that you're doing an *unpaid* internship. If you make it sound like you're going to be doing regular work, you could get turned away because you don't have a work visa.

In the next chapter, I'll discuss the next step in your development as an international worker and traveler—how to find permanent work overseas.

IVORY COAST

CHAPTER 4, VOL. I:

WORKING ABROAD

Intro

You may be thinking, "Okay, studying abroad I understand. You get cultural exposure, a more worthwhile experience and credit at your university. Interning abroad makes sense too—the internships are more challenging, they stand out on your resume. That all makes sense. But I'm not really planning to *work* abroad. I just want to use my international course or internship to get a job at home. Do I really need to know about working abroad?"

The world is changing, and the job market is changing along with it. The world is getting smaller, and with global communications being a reality in today's world, location is no longer a concern for many jobs. Opportunities are everywhere, and more companies than ever before are hiring people who are from other countries or living in other countries. That means you can live anywhere you want to, anywhere in the world, and have a successful career.

When looking for work, most people focus on just the area where they live—their town or city or metropolitan area. But the more you expand that circle, the more opportunities you'll find. That's a job-hunting advantage that's easy to access, because it's just about having the willingness to move somewhere else. And if your industry is being affected by a national economic downturn, you can escape that effect by looking overseas.

Most people think, "Okay, if you lose your job or it's hard to find work in your industry, you need to go back to school." That's the go-to alternative option—go back to school and get a new credential or some new skills. But that's not always easy to do. How do you know what you'll be good at, or where the demand will be, once you're out of school? It's much easier, and gives you just as much of an advantage, if you're willing to move to where the jobs are—or better yet, get the jobs to come to you by working remotely.

The power of knowing how to find work overseas is that it gives you options. It gives you flexibility. It allows you to find work that pays well, in your industry, rather than having to settle for whatever you can find in your city. If you're job hunting and not finding anything, you can fall into a "scarcity mindset," where you cave in to the pressure to make shortsighted decisions because they address your needs right now. If you do get a job offer while looking for work in your city, you may feel obligated to take it even if you already have concerns about it, or it doesn't pay quite enough, or it will be stressful and require long hours.

But once you include overseas jobs as an option, you realize that there are lots of jobs out there—and you become focused on finding the best one for you. You start looking for things like work/life balance and growth opportunities instead of (just enough) money and security. You hold out for a job that you're excited about, that will help move your career forward or support the life you want. That decision will boost your earning potential, your career path, and your general quality of life.

Around the time I was graduating, I was interviewing for corporate office jobs and none of them really excited me. I saw where I would end up long term, and that wasn't the road I wanted to take. Once I started looking for work abroad and saw all the possibilities that were out there, I became much more focused on jobs that could support my career path and my passion for traveling. Eventually I found my way to work remotely, which lets me travel, earn good money, and live wherever I want—something I didn't even think was possible when I was starting out.

For me, that first overseas job at the Czech University in Prague was a proof of concept. It showed me that I could do this, and that others were doing it too. Over time, I realized that I could take my approach to other countries and find work there too. I've now worked in Australia, Croatia, Czechia, Ireland, New Zealand, and South Korea, and while I am currently working remotely for an American company, I'm based in Medellín, Colombia.

Looking back, if I had taken an office job in the United States and stayed there, I think I would regret not having tried to travel and work abroad—even though I didn't realize how far I could take it at the time. I had a passion for travel, and I think it was important for me to try to pursue that. Over the years, I've built up memories and experiences with friends, mentors, and relationships that I've carried with me through so many different countries. I don't think I could have done that any other way but by traveling, seeing new things, and meeting new people. I truly feel that living and working abroad helped me figure out what I want to do, in general and professionally.

There's a common narrative structure in myths called the monomyth or the hero's journey, as described by mythologist Joseph Campbell. Movies and books today, like *Star Wars* and *Lord of the Rings*, follow this pattern, and it starts with the call to adventure. Something happens to interrupt the hero's ordinary life, and it takes him or her on a quest or a journey.

I would really like for this book to be your call to adventure. Each of us is the hero in our own life, and I want this to be the nudge or the interruption that encourages you to go out and start looking at traveling for yourself. I think traveling is a universal experience—or should be. It completely changes how you see the world and yourself, and it tends to give you a lot more confidence and openness.

When you're working and traveling abroad, there are more challenges, but your challenges become accomplishments, and your accomplishments become milestones. Look at the first time getting paid in another currency, for example. It's gratifying to overcome each challenge you run into and do things you didn't think you could. I don't think you get that same experience in your home country—it's a lot harder to push the envelope when you're completely comfortable and at home.

But another factor to consider is, what if you're not completely comfortable in your home country? In the United States, the stereotypical office job felt like something that was expected of me, and I wasn't thrilled about it. All it took was for me to go abroad and see other ways of living and working to convince me that I'd be happier working in another country than at home. As I've said before, Americans tend to make work the focus of our lives. We're not good at taking vacations, and it's common for people to be workaholics regardless of the type of job they have.

Traveling taught me a lot about how other countries approach work. Of the countries I've visited, I feel like Australia has the best work/life balance. It's a developed country, very productive with a high GDP, but Australians still travel and enjoy life to the fullest. Imagine living in a place where you aren't just allowed but are required to take four weeks of vacation time every year. This is common in Australia and New Zealand. Mandatory paid vacation is a real thing. I find that interesting, since Australia and New Zealand aren't even considered the front-runners for paid leave.

Having lived and worked in the United States and South Korea, and I would include Japan in this group as well, these are countries that have high productivity—but also a culture of being workaholics. I think there are serious downsides to that, not only for individuals but for the society as a whole. Traveling can help you gain a different perspective on some of the issues you may be facing at home and help you find a way of living that works better for you.

I don't want to discourage hard work, but there has to be a happy medium. A healthy balance has more benefits than you might imagine. Not only do you have the ability to have more experiences that enrich your life, but when it comes to work, it has been proven that a healthy work/life balance increases productivity and lowers work-related stress—which is beneficial to the immune system and reduces illnesses.

☐   KENYA

Getting Started

THE WORKING HOLIDAY VISA

You can start working abroad at any point in your career, and at any age, with or without a college degree, but it is easier if you're under thirty and have a university education. That's because the United States has reciprocal agreements with certain countries that people who meet the requirements, which typically include that a person be under thirty, can show up in these countries and get a "working holiday" visa, which will allow you to work there for up to a year. That's about the perfect amount of time to work in a country and decide if you like it, and you can often extend that period if you want.

Countries where Americans can easily get a working holiday visa include:

- New Zealand

- Australia

- Ireland

- Korea

- Singapore

Some of these countries allow you to apply for a working visa for free, while others might charge a fee. Either way, once you receive the visa, you can show up in that country ready to work immediately. One of the nice things about this visa is that you don't *have* to work the whole time. The rules change from country to country, but often you can only work for the same company for a certain amount of time, such as six months. There are ways to get around this—many companies can transfer you to one of their subsidiaries so you can continue working for them—but most travelers will work the six months, take a break to travel and visit more of the country, and then start another job.

WORKING VISA

If you're over 30, you will need a working visa, which usually requires company sponsorship. This means the company needs to prove that they need you, an American, to work for them because they can't fill the job with local applicants. This can create a bit of a barrier to entry, because you can't apply for work in the country unless you have a working visa, which you can't get unless you have a job (or job offer) from a company in that country. Generally, these regulations are set up with the intention of protecting the country's citizens from having their jobs taken away by foreign workers.

One simple way to navigate this is to go for an English teaching job in a non-English-speaking country. By definition, that's a job that they can't fill locally, so you're not taking a job away from a local worker. My only caution here is that many people don't know about the working holiday visa, so they go straight for the English teaching jobs as a way to visit the country. I definitely recommend that you start by exploring the working holiday visa if you're eligible, because that's an easier and less restrictive way to work in the country. If you're not eligible for it, teaching English is a good route to explore.

But even then, as I mentioned earlier, unless your career goal is to teach, think of the English teaching job as something to do for a year while working on your next career move. It's easy to stay in that role for multiple years, and then you can get a bit stuck and not know how to break out of it. So if you take an English teaching job and you already know you don't want to be a teacher long term, it's a good idea to make sure you're already working on your "exit strategy."

Transitioning between industries can be harder while working abroad because it can affect your working visa, so it's a good idea to carefully consider how a career change would affect your situation, and plan well in advance.

Regardless of what visa you have, one great way to transition between careers is through remote or freelance work. This is how I transitioned to my current situation, where I hold a tourist visa but I'm working remotely. Because I'm working for an American company, I'm not breaking any rules. Especially if you are over thirty, working online will let you retain the flexibility to live and work wherever you want, without a working holiday visa. One caveat is, most tourist visas are only good for about ninety days. So if you want to stay longer, you'll need to look at other options.

OTHER VISA OPTIONS

There are several different visas available, depending on the country, and it's important to research them if you're planning to stay in the country beyond ninety days. Your country of choice may have an "investment visa" available, where you purchase real estate (or something similar) and that allows you to stay. Even a student visa might work, depending on the hours of study that you have to put in. You never know what options they might have that could apply to your personal situation, so this is great information to look up in advance and keep in mind in case things change. You might think you only need a ninety-day tourist visa, but then you could fall in love with the country and need to figure out a way to stay.

Another option that can work for any age group is to explore dual citizenship or international residency. If your relatives have citizenship in another country, sometimes that will allow you to apply for citizenship in that country as well, and then you can carry two passports. This is definitely worth exploring because it would allow you to go to the country where you have citizenship and work just like anyone else, without needing a visa.

If you feel you need help navigating this process, you can always pay for a third-party visa service. In my opinion, the visa application process is generally not that bad. I handled all my own paperwork for my visas in the countries where I've worked—but it can take some time to actually find work. There are some services that offer to handle the visa process and help you with job placement. They never guarantee anything, but if you're in a specialized field or looking for something specific, these services can really cut down your job-hunting time.

Once You're There, the Initiation

First things first: you'll need to find somewhere to sleep! If you can stay with a local friend, that's ideal. If not, I would recommend finding a hostel, especially if you're under thirty and traveling on a working holiday visa. At the hostel, you will usually be able to meet a lot of people doing the same thing as you, and you'll be able to start building a network. Your fellow hostel-stayers should be able to tell you what staffing firms are worth checking out, which local companies they've worked for, and maybe even some job introductions.

If the idea of a hostel doesn't appeal to you, you can treat it as a short-term solution while looking for an apartment or shared accommodations. There are even women-only hostels or rooms, if that is a concern, and you can usually get a locker for your valuables, so there are ways to make it workable and to accommodate any concerns you might have. Hostels are not for everyone. There's not much privacy or personal space, and it can be challenging to stick to a routine of getting up early and going to work. But because of the low cost, and the built-in network you can often find there, it can really be worth trying, at least for your first few weeks in a new country. I always preferred to stay at a hostel when I arrived in a new country and was looking for work. Once I found work, I would find something a little more private like an apartment or Airbnb. These were typically shared accommodations with roommates, which I would find by word of mouth through work or by looking online.

To find work, there are usually local staffing firms that

you can find and sign up with, and I would definitely recommend going that route—particularly if you're looking for work in a non-English-speaking country. You can use Google to find the top twenty or so staffing firms in that country or city, and fill out an application with each one. Try to set up in-person interviews with these firms, as this tends to show that you're eager to find work. Once that process is completed, you have twenty people looking for work for you. They will tend to find you opportunities suited to your skill set and career path, and a bonus is that they will often be temporary roles—maybe six months or so—which is perfect if you have a working holiday visa or if you just want to work for a short time, save up, and then go traveling.

Once you've found a place to stay and work, you'll need to start building a community for yourself. I love websites that help you find shared-interest groups or events, because you can find people who have something in common with you right away. General networking and socializing events are other good options, where you show up at a bar and there are fifty or more people there to talk to.

When it comes to working abroad, the most important things are to be aware of your priorities and plan accordingly. If your focus is on finding a good career opportunity and starting work right away, a good plan would be to head for the largest city in the country or the capital city, since it will have the best job opportunities. If you do find a good job opportunity, it's important to make sure you take it seriously. Some people see overseas work as a hobby or just a way to fund travel. This book, however, is for people who are thinking of these jobs in the same way I do—as career moves, just like they would be at home.

No matter what job I had, I was engaged with my work, and I saw each job in terms of what it could add to my resume, what kind of work experience I was gaining, and whether I was building connections with people who could be references or who could give a recommendation. And then travel was something that I did on my own time, between jobs or during my time off. So if you really want to develop your career with overseas work, make sure you're ready to show your employer that this job is your priority.

On the other hand, if travel is your priority, I think the best thing for you is to recognize that and take some time when you arrive to travel and look around. In fact, if you have the money to support yourself for a month or two when you arrive in a new country, it could be a great idea to visit different cities and find a city you really like, so you can focus your job hunt on that area. This also helps get that "travel bug" out of your system, so when you're ready to find work, you can make that your focus.

Often when I arrived in a country, I needed to find work right away, so I just headed straight for the biggest city and started my job hunt immediately. In general, the biggest cities will have the most to offer newcomers. They'll have the most job openings, the best entertainment and nightlife, and the biggest expat communities. At the same time, if you have friends or relatives in a smaller city, that could make a big difference; having that support system is huge. So traveling to different cities, if you have the time and money, can sometimes help you figure out where you actually want to be.

It's also worth remembering that you're moving to a new country, where they may have a different take on work/life balance from what you're used to, and this can be a good opportunity to take some time to enjoy yourself. If you were working sixty to seventy hours a week at a job in the United States and you didn't like it, maybe you don't need to hunt for full-time work right away in another country. Maybe you'd rather take some time to relax and decide what you want to do next. Along those lines, you could also consider part-time or temporary work for your first overseas job. That will leave you time for adapting to the new country, settling in, and just experiencing your new environment. After all, you're there to enjoy life, so make time to do just that!

When you're ready to look for work, you'll want to make sure your resume and cover letter are the best quality possible. After all, you are looking for genuinely good career opportunities, whether they are full time and permanent, part time, or temporary. If you are still in college, your school likely offers career counseling and resume-writing services, where they'll have you provide all your work information and help you present it in the best way. If not, it's worth finding a career counseling or resume-writing service on your own to get help with this. And once you have a resume and cover letter that are formatted for the United States, I would highly recommend that you research the formatting that is most common in your new country, and create another resume in that format. Overseas companies do tend to accommodate American-style resumes, but it definitely helps to show that you did the research and figured out how to present the information in the local format.

Another tip for resumes is that many countries outside of North America require a photo. So it'll help to be prepared with professional-looking headshots to send along with your resume. These don't have to be fancy, as long as you look professional in the photo. You can take one yourself or have a friend take it for you, but it would probably be a good idea to have this ready before you leave.

Transitioning to Build Your Career

The first thing you need to build your career is a job that aligns with your career goals. Then, the main thing is to prioritize your relationships with your boss and employer. Obviously, you should also try to excel at your job as much as possible, but often that's just the foundation. You also need to be able to network effectively and build a positive relationship with your boss and other stakeholders. Many companies are open to keeping overseas workers permanently, but it's a bigger investment for them compared to local workers, so you must prove your worth.

If you are planning to move to another country or transition out of your current industry after a year or two, consider carefully to make sure that you're going to be able to build on your progress. That you'll be able to find a job that will be the next step on your career path, and that your current work experience will translate well for the job market in your next country. With some research and planning, you can make sure your career progresses with your next move, and you're never starting over at zero.

I highly recommend remote and freelance work as a way to transition into a new industry, particularly if you are over thirty because you don't have the option of getting a working holiday visa to make things easier. There are online platforms where freelancers and clients can find each other and set up contracts, and these can be great to pursue as weekend projects, so you can get started in your new industry without having to give up your current job. Then you can gradually put in more hours and take on more clients until you're ready to go off on your own, or until you've built up enough work experience, or enough of a portfolio, that you can effectively job hunt in your new industry.

Part of the reason remote work is so helpful is because it is difficult to change careers as a foreign worker in another country, and even more difficult to arrive in a country on a tourist visa and then find work and transition to a work visa. It generally doesn't happen that way. If you're already on a working visa, local recruiters and staffing agencies may be able to help you find another job. But really, if you can take your career transition online, it will make your life a lot easier because you won't have to worry about violating regulations.

I've mentioned the term "digital nomad," and for the purposes of this book, it just means someone who can work anywhere as long as they have a laptop and Wi-Fi. If you research freelancer websites or remote job platforms, you'll find dozens—or even hundreds—of skill sets that are being used to work online, from the usual digital careers like programming and web design, all the way to traditional office jobs like accounting and law. If you don't think of your skill set as something that can be done online, it's worth researching it—because freelance and remote work are some of the fastest-growing segments of the job market.

If you are a very social person and thrive on face-to-face contact, you will find that remote work doesn't automatically provide this. You may need to take steps to arrange social opportunities for yourself by being more deliberate about making time for friends, or finding space to work outside of your home. Sometimes working in a coffee shop, an outdoor area, or a coworking space can be a big help for remote workers who need social contact. You will also need to find the routine that allows you to be most productive. Some people can easily work from home, while others need to go to a public working space. Some people can work in their pajamas, while others need to get fully dressed to switch into their "working mode." If you can start working remotely while you're still at home, either for a company or as a freelancer, you'll have a better idea of what kind of working space will work for you when you go overseas.

I believe the benefits of remote work far outweigh any negatives. There's no commute to take up your time, for one thing. Clients tend to judge you only on the quality of the work and whether it was done within the time and budget constraints. They don't worry so much about standard office-job metrics like punctuality, looking busy, and always having the right kind of attitude. It can be a really nice escape from office politics, which is extremely stressful for a lot of people. It cuts down on your budget for clothing, transportation, and food, since you don't need special "work" clothes, a car, or packed lunches for the office.

Working remotely in another country also gives you the freedom to explore and enjoy the new culture, as I mentioned earlier. But if you are not focused on working for pay, and you would rather find another way to be productive while traveling, there are options for that, too. There are volunteer organizations you can get involved with, and websites that will connect you with people who run farms where you can work in exchange for room and board. Those are options that will let you work and learn, but you can do them on a tourist visa because it's not for pay. Another option is to go into business for yourself. Whether you freelance online or create your own company (that's registered in the United States), either option could allow you to work and travel on a tourist visa while having the freedom to learn and explore on your own terms.

There are tons of online resources for finding remote work. When you search the term "remote work," I highly recommend that you add the name of the city where you are or want to work (for instance, type "Sydney, Australia remote work"). It's not always necessary, but there are many companies that will want to meet you and know that you live locally, even though the work will be done remotely. You can also search for local groups of freelancers or online entrepreneurs, and again include the city name, to find groups to join and start networking.

One of the best benefits about remote work is that it allows you to earn money in one currency and pay your bills in another. For example, since I work for an American company, I'm paid in American dollars. But since I live in Colombia, I pay my expenses in pesos. This type of situation can boost your purchasing power and allow you a better quality of life or accelerated saving. It's definitely a factor to consider if you're thinking about remote work in a different country. It all depends on the cost of living. In some countries, you can get a nicely furnished apartment, utilities, groceries, and even luxuries like a private chef, chauffeur, and maids all for less than US$1,500 a month. Or you can skip the luxuries and have more money for savings or more traveling!

Final Thoughts

The main thing to know about working abroad is that it does take some planning and forethought. It's a fantastic option that will expand your job market, potentially upgrade your skills and experience, and allow you to live wherever you want. But it requires you to know your goals and to figure out how to make it work for the country where you want to be. I'll discuss this in more detail in the next chapter.

CHAPTER 4, VOL. II:

WORKING ABROAD

Options and Opportunities

In this chapter, I'll discuss some of the ways to get started working abroad. This is not an exhaustive list, but I still think you'll find there are more options than you were expecting, and that one or two (or more) of these options will stick out to you as things that you could actually pull off. Because this way of life is completely normal for many people all over the world, and once you really start to look at the ways we do it, you'll see that it's also possible for you.

All the information in this section is current as of December 2018. Throughout this chapter, there are details that are subject to change without notice, especially related to the specifics of certain visas or immigration programs. When specified, these details are always shown in bullet lists. On my website, globalcareerbook.com, you will find up-to-date versions of these lists, which are useful for reference as you start to compare countries and make plans.

Once you're really serious about going to a specific country, you will need to double-check everything using the website for that country's embassy or consulate, where you can verify all the details either online or by contacting someone. As always, when it comes to something as significant as moving to another country, it's important to do your own research and check your information thoroughly before finalizing your plans.

Working Holiday Visa (WHV)

If you are under thirty and considering living and working abroad, you need to know about the Working Holiday program (a.k.a. working holiday visa), which I mentioned earlier. This program is in effect all over the world and is one of the easiest ways to find work in another country.

You can find up-to-date details on working holiday visas and application links on this page: globalcareerbook. com/whv.

In essence, the United States has reciprocal agreements with specific countries, including:

New Zealand   Australia   Ireland

South Korea   Singapore

☐   MALAYSIA

These agreements allow for citizens—primarily young people—to travel between these countries to work and live on a short-term basis. Most of these countries are English speaking, so the cultural transition is easier. But most importantly, the visa process is simplified and less expensive, and those countries generally have strong job markets. There are five or six criteria you need to meet, which are related to:

- Cost (application fee)

- Age (typically applicants have to be under thirty)

- Length of stay (six to twelve months, depending on the country)

- Funds you can access (i.e., bank account balance)

- Health requirements as applicable

- Educational requirements as applicable

A working holiday visa is perfectly aligned with the lifestyle that I've described in this book; you can live in a country for six months or a year (depending on the country), study, work, and travel. In this section, I'm going to discuss each of the WHV countries currently available, what they require, and what it's like to live and work there.

First, as I said, there are some requirements you have to meet when you apply. The requirements are designed to make sure you're using the program for its stated purpose and that you're healthy, able to take care of yourself financially, and planning to exit the country when your visa expires. The exact requirements vary from country to country, but most applications will require you to state and/or prove that you:

- have a specified minimum bank account balance (I recommend US$5,000, though the requirement is often lower);

- have booked your departure flight or have enough money to do so;

- are a college or university student or have recently graduated; and

- are free from diseases such as HIV/AIDS, yellow fever, tuberculosis, etc.

Whether or not you're asked to produce evidence that you meet these requirements will depend on your specific circumstances. In my own experience, sometimes I had to prove my bank account balance and sometimes I didn't. Sometimes I was asked to provide x-rays (to rule out tuberculosis) and sometimes I wasn't asked for any medical documentation. There is also a "good character" requirement, which essentially lets them ask you to produce a background check or police records (I was never asked for this).

There are a few additional constraints to be aware of. Some countries place restrictions on the industries you can work in, and some countries have a limit on the number of WHVs, which means they stop giving out the visas once that limit (sometimes called a "quota") is met. This information should be available before you apply, so keep an eye out for it when you're reviewing the country's government website. In general, the WHV can't be extended to children or a spouse. So if you want to travel with family, you'll need to find visas for them outside of the WHV program (probably tourist visas).

Here are the countries that you can currently visit on a WHV:

NEW ZEALAND

New Zealand is probably one of the most beautiful countries, per square mile, that I've ever been to. There's a reason all the *Lord of the Rings* movies were filmed there. The people are open and friendly, and the country has incredible biodiversity. Everything about New Zealand makes it easy to travel to and enjoy your stay. They don't even have any dangerous insects or reptiles, like Australia does—the worst they have is horseflies.

Much like Australia, the people in New Zealand are very laid back, culturally speaking. Their work culture is as productive as any other developed nation's, but they just have this relaxed approach to life that I really appreciated.

While I was there, I was in Auckland, which is comparable in terms of living expenses to any major American city (so, a bit expensive). But if you go out to the smaller towns, it does become more affordable.

Overall, it's a very easy transition to move from the United States to New Zealand, though there are a few minor practical differences. For example, in New Zealand (and Australia), payroll and bills are on a weekly cycle—you pay weekly rent and receive a weekly paycheck. If you want to see more of the country, it's a good idea to rent a car—but you'll notice that they drive on the left side of the road. And you'll need an adapter for your American electronics. That's about it. Really, there's nothing too crazy in terms of adjusting to a new country.

I also found that New Zealand had one of the easiest visa application processes. It took me about an hour to complete the forms and apply online. That's *really* fast. There was no fee, and they only required me to have about US$3,000 in my bank account. They did require me to show proof that I either had a departure flight booked or money to buy one. Because of this (it's a standard requirement), I would recommend booking a round-trip ticket—and make sure the dates are flexible. It's often cheaper to book a round trip anyway, and it will just be one less thing to plan while you're there.

Some of the best resources for finding work in New Zealand are:

- seek.co.nz (this is where I found my job)

- trademe.co.nz/jobs (similar to craigslist)

- careers.govt.nz (large job database)

- globalcareerbook.com/jobs (remote and international job board)

You can find an up-to-date list of all the resources, tips, and links at globalcareerbook.com/whv.

☐   MARSHALL ISLANDS

WHV Info

Costs: $0 for Americans

Age: 18–30 years old; no dependents or children

Length of Visa: 12 months (must have proof of onward travel or enough money to buy a ticket; they make random checks)

Funding (bank account balance): US$3,000 (occasional random checks)

Educational Requirements: None specified

Health Requirements: Must have travel insurance, may be asked for x-rays or other medical information

Other Information: Quota is unlimited, easy online application, processed within a few weeks

Once you arrive in New Zealand, all the same techniques that I discussed earlier for finding work and settling in apply. You can start by researching the biggest staffing firms and applying to them for temporary work or office jobs. You can also look for online or remote work, which I will soon discuss at greater length. Get started building a local network by staying at a hostel and making friends with the other travelers staying there. I will also discuss ways to find online or remote work in this chapter; once you have a remote job, you can really go anywhere you want, which will open up so many possibilities.

AUSTRALIA

Something that I still find amazing about Australia is that 90 percent of the population lives on the coast. Essentially, all the major towns and cities are near the beach, which makes Australia amazing for surfing and spending time near the ocean. If you venture into the area in the center of the continent, you will encounter the world-famous Outback. Often, tour guides in the Outback will be Aboriginal Australians, and they can tell you a lot about their history and culture. Aboriginal Australians are thought to have one of the oldest civilizations on Earth, and historians believe they may have arrived in Australia more than 60,000 years ago. There are amazing tours, camps, workshops, and museums dedicated to Aboriginal Australian culture.

Australia also has amazing wildlife, like koalas and kangaroos, as well as many varieties of snakes and spiders. Australia is home to several dangerous animals, like sharks, alligators, box jellyfish, and venomous spiders and snakes. It's fascinating if you're into reptiles or bugs (there's a centipede that can grow large enough to feed on mice and lizards!) … and maybe less fascinating if you're not. But the truth is that statistically, you're pretty safe. Shark deaths, for example, are incredibly rare (the Australian Shark Attack Annual Report indicates there was one shark-related death in 2017). You do have to be careful about where you swim, but that's just part of the culture. Everyone else at the beach will know where to swim and not swim, so it's not hard to figure out.

MAURITIUS

One appealing aspect of Australia is that it's south of the equator, so it's warm year-round. Sydney does get a little colder in the winter, but you can always travel up north and find a nice beach spot—experience summer all year!

In terms of working in Australia, I found they have the best work/life balance of any of the countries where I worked. They make work an enjoyable experience, and most people build good social relationships with their coworkers. So it feels a lot different from working in the United States, where your coworkers kind of get along but probably don't go out of their way to see each other outside of work. Both Australia and New Zealand also have mandatory vacations. If you go for a year without taking your vacation time, they'll make you stop working, and you have to take your vacation before you can come back. That's just an example of how those cultures are structured and how they really emphasize people enjoying life, as opposed to people making sacrifices for work. There are still demanding jobs and jobs that require overtime, but those tend to be the exception rather than the rule, and they tend to pay accordingly. It's kind of an eye-opener when you experience a work culture that is very different from what you grew up with, and you realize how many different ways there are to balance work and life.

Living expenses in Australia can be higher than in the United States—significantly higher in Sydney. Alcohol is especially expensive. Both Australia and New Zealand are big wine producers, so drinking local wines is one of the best options. While I was there, I found that free Wi-Fi is not common, which was a bit of a shock compared to other countries, especially America. So if you do work remotely and you prefer to work in coffee shops or similar types of places, that's definitely something to keep in mind.

Some of the best resources for finding work in Australia are:

- seek.com.au (most professional and serious job board)

- gumtree.com.au/jobs (this is where I found my job)

- jobsearch.gov.au/job (large job database funded by the government)

- globalcareerbook.com/jobs (remote and international job board)

You can find an up-to-date list of all the resources, tips, and links at globalcareerbook.com/whv.

WHV Info

Costs: US$360

Age: 18–30 (inclusive); no dependents or children

Length of Visa: 12 months from date of entry

Funding (bank account balance): US$3,800 (AU$5,000)

Educational Requirements: High school diploma

Health Requirements: Must be free from diseases that are a "threat to public health," by which they mean serious diseases such as tuberculosis, HIV/ hepatitis, yellow fever, polio, and Ebola. This generally means producing a vaccination certificate, x-ray, or other evidence if requested.

Other Information: You can only hold this visa once; any subsequent applications will be denied.

IRELAND

The Irish are very welcoming people, and there is a close connection between Ireland and the United States. In 2013, the U.S. Census Bureau conducted a survey and found that there were about 33 million Americans with Irish ancestry, compared to an actual Irish population of about 4.7 million at the time.

The Irish countryside is stunning—lush and green—and what's nice about Ireland is that it's a fairly accessible country. It's really easy to travel by car, so if you're there for a year, you can see all of it if you want to. There are major cities, like Dublin and Cork, and if you're driving, there are two major coastal trails—the Wild Atlantic Way (west coast of Ireland) and the Causeway Coastal Route—which are both breathtaking.

The Irish have a rich cultural history, and they still celebrate their Gaelic roots. You will see street signs in English and Gaelic, for example. Gaelic is taught in Irish schools, so most people can say a few phrases, and some speak it fluently.

Practically speaking, Ireland tends to be more expensive than what you might be used to in America. But in any country, this is only an issue until you find work. Then, of course, you'll be making the local currency and will find it easier to cover your expenses.

Some of the best resources for finding work in Ireland are:

- jobs.ie (largest selection of jobs in Ireland)

- irishjobs.ie (another large selection of jobs)

MONACO

- globalcareerbook.com/jobs (remote and international job board)

You can find an up-to-date list of all the resources, tips, and links at globalcareerbook.com/whv.

WHV Info

Costs: Approx. US$350

Age: Over 18

Length of Visa: 12 months

Funding (bank account balance): Minimum US$4,000

Educational Requirements: Must be enrolled in or have graduated from a postsecondary study program (i.e., college or university) within the past 12 months

Health Requirements: Must hold medical/travel insurance

Other Information: This visa can be held more than once, as long as you still meet all the conditions. When you land in Ireland, you need to register with the Immigration Bureau and pay an additional fee of $400.

SOUTH KOREA

I found that South Korea does an outstanding job of exporting their culture, much like Hollywood does for the United States. K-pop and Korean soap operas are world famous. So some aspects of the culture were familiar to me right off the bat because of that cultural exposure—particularly their music and entertainment.

A significant part of the Korean experience is food. One of the most common types of food, called kimchi, is fermented cabbage. They've been making it for thousands of years, and you can't have a meal in Korea without being served kimchi.

Korea is about 70 percent mountains, so it has great hiking trails, and hiking is very much a part of Korean culture. You'll go for a hike and be passed by eighty-year-old grandmothers who have been hiking their entire lives. Another substantial aspect of Korean culture is the nightlife; they love to go out, drink, and have dinner late in the evening. So if you're in a Korean city, there's never any shortage of things to do at night. The overall culture is considerably different from the culture here in the United States, making a unique experience.

Traveling within Korea is quite simple because they have amazing transportation infrastructure. Their transit system is the nicest I've ever seen, and you can effectively get around the city or country just using public transit.

They also have the fastest internet service in the world. It's one of the things you notice when you're there—they have extremely advanced technology, and it all just works. I will say that finding a non-teaching job can be very hard, but not impossible.

Some of the best resources for finding non-teaching work in South Korea are:

- seoul.craigslist.co.kr (very active and the best place for foreigners to find jobs)

- LinkedIn and Facebook groups (the next best place to look for jobs)

- globalcareerbook.com/jobs (remote and international job board)

You can find an up-to-date list of all the resources, tips, and links at globalcareerbook.com/whv.

WHV Info

Costs: US$45

Age: 18–30 (inclusive)

Length of Visa: 18 months for Americans

Funding (bank account balance): Roughly US$3,000

Educational Requirements: Americans must either be postsecondary students or have graduated within the last 12 months (proof is required)

Health Requirements: For United States citizens, none

Other Information: There is a limit of 2,000 WHV holders in the country at any given time. This visa can only be held once. Once in the country, you must register with the Immigration Office and pay a fee of about US$300. There are a number of professions that are barred from entry for WHV holders—including foreign language instruction, which is under a different visa.

SINGAPORE

I think a major draw to Singapore is that it's centrally located among the southeast Asian countries, including Vietnam, Malaysia, Philippines, and Indonesia. Those countries are all so close together that the flights between them are extremely inexpensive. It *is* expensive to fly from the United States to Singapore, but once you're there, you can go on short, inexpensive trips to other countries that wouldn't normally be as accessible, kind of like taking the trains in Europe. For example, it's common to find flights from Singapore to Malaysia for under $20.

This is different from Australia and New Zealand, which are both a little more isolated. Singapore is highly technologically advanced, much like South Korea, and it's also one of the more expensive countries to live in. However, since the visa is only for six months, you could definitely work just for that time, and then travel around the region once your visa is expired.

Some of the best resources for finding non-teaching work in South Korea are:

- stjobs.sg (professional job board)

- singapore.craigslist.com (lots of options, but some are low quality)

- gumtree.sg (similar to craigslist)

- globalcareerbook.com/jobs (remote and international job board)

You can find an up-to-date list of all the resources, tips, and links at globalcareerbook.com/whv.

WHV Info

Costs: US$150

Age: 18–25

Length of Visa: 6 months

Funding (bank account balance): Unknown

Educational Requirements: Undergraduate or graduate from a recognized university in Australia, France, Germany, Hong Kong, Japan, New Zealand, Switzerland, United Kingdom, or United States

Health Requirements: None listed

Other Information: Like South Korea, Singapore has a quota of 2,000 WHV holders at any time, and their Work Holiday website will notify you if the program is full. This visa is not renewable.

Visa Options for Travelers over Thirty

The first part of this chapter focuses on travelers under thirty years of age because it's important to know about the specific, structured programs for that age group. The over-thirty crowd has just as many possibilities open to them, though sometimes it requires a little creativity to find the best option for you.

Outside of the WHV program, the best plan depends on your goals. If you want to travel from country to country, then you won't want to go through the process of getting a working permit. Instead, you should try to stay on a tourist visa. However, depending on the country, there can be a lot of other options available. If you want to move to another country, get a job there, and stay for a longer period of time, there are ways to do that, too.

Examples of Non-Working Visas around the World

Here, I'm going to list a few sample countries from around the world and their visa options (outside of a work visa). This shows you that there are a wide variety of visas available, and as you read through the list, you will start to see why I said this process can involve getting "creative." Many of these options are more flexible than you might expect, so it just requires a little out-of-the-box thinking to figure out how to get one of them to work for you. There are also resources for you, such as lawyers and visa services, that will help you navigate through all the information, identify your best options, and carry out the exact steps to get your visa approved. Doing your research is the first step, but this can be an involved process for some of the more complex visas. Just know that you don't have to figure it all out by yourself—you can easily find help. You can access the free tool here, which tell you exactly which visa is required for visiting another country: globalcareerbook.com/visas.

Note: This information is accurate as of December 2018. Visa regulations change frequently, but there are always new and creative ways to stay long term in countries.

COLOMBIA

- *Tourist Visa*: 180 days for Americans in a calendar year (extension required after 90 days)

NEW ZEALAND

- *Medical Visa*: 1+ year (even for things like braces/ Invisalign)

- *Student Visa*: 1+ year for studying Spanish or other subjects (online classes are an option, too)

- *Business Visa*: Small investment to start business; after 5 years, eligible for residency

- *Investor Visa*: Approx. $100,000 property purchase; after 5 years, eligible for residency

- *Civil Partnership Visa*: 2+ years and for people with a partner

- *Retiree Visa*: Proof of pension

In this list of Colombian visa options, some details might have stuck out to you. Notice that the medical visa can be used for nonsurgical procedures, such as braces and Invisalign, while the student visa can be qualified for with online classes a few hours a month. Either of those options could fit into your remote working schedule very easily. The civil partnership visa gets a little more complicated, as you need to provide proof that you and your partner are living as a couple, and it's more or less the equivalent of getting married.

The business and investor visas are also a little more complicated; you would need to research exactly what kind of investments or business ventures would be eligible. It is highly recommended to use a local lawyer or visa service before obtaining any investor or business visa. The retiree option requires proof of pension, which would most likely include government pensions and Social Security.

I really recommend considering Colombia if you are working remotely for a company that pays in American dollars (or, really, any Western currency); your money will go extremely far, and you'll be able to have a highly comfortable life. Colombia is also convenient for remote workers because it's in line with US time zones, making it much easier to work on an American company's schedule. Not to mention, the weather is perfect, particularly around Medellin; they call it "the eternal spring"—a.k.a. 75 degrees year-round.

MEXICO

- *Tourist Visa*: 180 days for Americans

- *Temporary Resident Visa (FM3)*: 3–4 years; must prove monthly income of $1,500–2,000

- *Permanent Resident Visa*: No expiration; must prove monthly income of $2,500–3,000

Mexico is another great location for remote work because it's so accessible to the United States, with frequent flights available. Like Colombia, it's also in line with the same time zones as the United States. You could easily maintain a close working relationship with an American company while you're located in Mexico, with convenient flights and compatible work schedules. There are also extensive expat communities in Playa del Carmen and Mexico City.

NIGER

What's worth noting about the Mexican visas is that they are based on duration and income. So the tourist visa, which is good for six months for Americans, would be good for short-term travel. The temporary resident visa would be good for remote working, and the permanent resident visa would suit a retiree or someone, of course, looking to permanently relocate.

THAILAND

- *Tourist Visa*: 30 days, but can easily be extended

- *Elite VIP Visa*: 5–10–20 years for around $3,000 per year; priority treatment at immigration

- *Self-Defense Education Visa*: 1 year or longer; for taking self-defense courses (costs around $1,000 for visa)

- *Retirement Visa*: Must be over 50 years old and have a steady income

The American dollar probably goes further in Thailand than anywhere else on this list, and you can afford a high quality of life there on an average American income. Thailand also has high-speed internet—even faster than what you can get in the United States. It's a misconception that developing countries don't have good infrastructure or technology. Particularly in the case of the internet, where that infrastructure is relatively new, Thailand has been building fast and is definitely on par with the United States, if not better.

When you think of moving to Thailand, some of the barriers that might come up in your mind might be things like, "The culture will be different, the language will be different, it won't feel like home." But in my experience, the strongest American expat communities are in those countries where the culture and language are completely different, because there is a need for people to find others they share common ground with. And there is a vibrant expat community in Thailand. You won't have a hard time meeting people.

When it comes to Thailand, the tourist visa is *very* easily renewed. Travelers often do what's called a "visa run" where they take a bus to the border, cross, and then immediately return. Their passport gets stamped, and their thirty days begins again. This does become inconvenient after a while, even if you extend your visa to sixty days, so the VIP visa is designed for people who want to stay on a longer tourist visa. But if you're new to the country, it's great to start with the thirty days. Take your time and learn the country before committing to a longer stay.

The self-defense visa is clearly meant for tourists who want to learn Thai boxing or other martial arts, as Thailand is known for them. To qualify for this visa, you just need to take martial arts classes once or twice a week.

PHILIPPINES

- *Tourist Visa*: 30 days, but easy to extend

- *Student Visa*: Must be studying

- *Retiree Visa*: At least 35 years old, must have a deposit of $20,000–50,000 (and show proof every 2 years)

NORTHERN IRELAND

The Philippines and America have close ties, and the governments have created fairly loose long-term visas that allow Americans to stay long term. It is easy to extend tourist visas and stay longer in the Philippines than in many other countries. The list I've provided shows just some of the many ways to stay long term in the Philippines.

CZECHIA

- *Long-Term Student Visa*

- *Long-Term Business Visa*

The EU is very strict when it comes to visas, and the process varies for each country. Living long term in the Czechia is possible, but it requires a bit of work. The most common option is to get a long-term business visa. This process is a bit more complicated for Czechia than other countries but still very possible to obtain. This visa is suitable for freelancers or self-employed people and is the most common for digital nomads. The other option is to obtain a student visa and study the Czech language a few times a week.

GEORGIA

- *Passport only for 365 days*

For those of you not familiar with Georgia, it's not only one of the fifty states, it's also a country at the intersection of Europe and Asia. This is a really interesting former Soviet country that is near the Black Sea and next to Turkey.

The country of Georgia has an extremely relaxed visa

policy and allows visitors to stay up to one year with little hassle or documentation. All you need is proof of health insurance and a passport, and you are able to stay in the country long term.

In the next section, I discuss options outside of the WHV program. In the introduction, I mentioned that I want to convince readers that it is *possible* to live and work abroad for years, so that when opportunities to do arise, they actually recognize them and seize them. Below are some potential opportunities that might be present or opening up in your life.

OPPORTUNITY #1:

Remote Work or Freelancing Online

I mentioned in the previous chapter that the online skills marketplace is expanding rapidly, and all kinds of work is being done online now. If your current skills aren't compatible with online work, you can always learn new ones with inexpensive online courses or bootcamps, and online work will give you a way to polish and develop those skills, even if it's just as a side venture until you're ready to go full time. Studies show that we learn new skills better when we're able to put them to work right away, and online work will allow you to do that while keeping your day job until you're ready to take the leap.

Remote and freelancing work, as long as you're paid online and not working for a local company, will allow you to live in any country on a tourist visa instead of a working permit. To find online work in a specific country or city (because sometimes you need to be based in a given location even though it's remote work), one trick I love is to search Facebook for "[City Name] + expats," "[City Name] + digital nomads," "[City Name] + entrepreneurs," etc. The results will show you relevant Facebook groups where you will often find people who are actually hiring for a wide range of jobs (marketing, sales, SEO).

I've just discussed most of the options for how to live in a country while working remotely. You can start with the standard tourist visa and extend it. Finding online work is easy, and there are tons of platforms, including upwork. com, freelancer.com, and toptal.com, and you can find my platform of online and international jobs at globalcareer-book.com/jobs.

OPPORTUNITY #2:

Large International Organizations (Accenture, P&G, EY, etc.) with Offices Worldwide

If you currently hold an office job at a large corporation, or you are in an industry or have a skill set that lends itself to working for large companies (for example, law or accounting), there might be a way to travel and work abroad without even leaving your day job.

This is a fairly common option for people who work at multinational companies that have offices all over the world, including the United States. Once you're working for the company, you can request a transfer to go to another country and work there, on either a temporary or full-time basis. If you are already contemplating a job change for other reasons, you could include in your job hunt companies with worldwide offices, where you could transfer internally. Another option is to talk with your current manager about transitioning your job to an online role. I've met quite a few young professionals who do this, sometimes using a small 10–15 percent pay decrease as incentive for the company if you really need more bargaining power. This percentage can easily be redeemed since living overseas can cut expenses in half.

OPPORTUNITY #3:

Working on a Cruise Ship

If you work in entertainment, hospitality, or customer service, cruise work can be a fantastic upgrade from the usual retail or service jobs in the United States. But cruise ships don't only need customer service staff. There is a huge range of jobs available, so it's always worth checking out.

Working on a cruise ship comes with room and board and full amenities, a built-in community of coworkers, and of course, the chance to see the world. It is real work, and it's not for everyone, but it can be a great way to develop your skills, meet new people, and live a little differently for a while.

OPPORTUNITY #4:

ESL + Transition to Another Career

Particularly in South Korea and Asia, it can be relatively easy to get a working visa as an English teacher. This does usually require a university or college degree, and English and teaching degrees are especially valuable. Assuming this isn't your long-term career goal, you can start planning your transition once you arrive, as you work and learn the culture.

OPPORTUNITY #5:

Volunteer or WWOOFing

Volunteering allows you to gain work and life experience with a tourist visa, since you're not working for pay. WWOOFing was mentioned in chapter 1. It's where you volunteer on organic farms all over the world in exchange for room and board. It's hard work, often physical labor, but can be a really rewarding way to live—and you don't need a college degree. You can find opportunities through WWOOF.org. Volunteering allows you to travel the world for a very low cost, since room and board are often covered by the organization you volunteer for. The lower your costs are, the longer you can live and travel, so it's not uncommon for people to volunteer or WWOOF for a year or more, traveling to different locations around the world, living on modest savings. The same amount of money you would need to move to another country (US$3,000–5,000) could probably also pay for months—or even a year—of volunteer travel. This is one example of how accessible this lifestyle can really be. While I've focused on ways to work and earn money abroad, if you want to take time off work and just travel, it's very easy to do that too.

Conclusion

What it all adds up to is that whatever your specific goal is, or your reason for wanting to be in a given country, chances are there's a way to do it. Whether you're under or over thirty, whether you have a college degree and a digital skill set or a conventional office or service job, or no degree at all, it's just a matter of looking through the visa options and the potential opportunities I've described and finding something that works for your situation. If your intention is to live in a country and spend money there, that's something any country will want to facilitate if they can.

They also know that the easier things are for immigrants, the more likely others will come and live there, too. That's because word of mouth is still the best way to find out which countries are easiest to move to. Finding expat communities in those countries and asking them your questions is a great strategy for figuring out where you'd like to go next. Another major factor is cost of living, especially if you're doing remote work. Thailand and the Philippines are very popular for this reason. The cost of living is very low, so you can afford a good quality of life and still set money aside every month.

In the next chapter, I'll discuss specific tips and advice for transitioning from a tourist to an expat and how to make your life even easier as you transition to living and working abroad.

CHAPTER 5:

THE EXPAT LIFE

Intro

Who is an expat? The formal definition is anyone who is living outside their native country. To me, it means anyone who is traveling in another country with an intention to put down roots and join a local community. Because that's the difference between living and traveling—when you start to make that place your home.

In this chapter, I'll discuss some ways to get started and build an expat life, both in terms of practical logistics and ways of thinking about it. I'll talk about how to find and build your community, what challenges to be prepared for, and why it's all worth it in the end.

I think it really sank in for me that I was an expat once I started to make friends—both local friends and friends in the expat community. I just kind of realized, "I'm part of this community. I have friends from all over the city, and I have local friends who grew up here." Because it's often easier to make expat friends, when I recognized that I also had local friends, I realized that I had built a local community around myself. I was an expat.

Becoming a Community Member

When you're looking at countries to settle in, I recommend checking out Facebook to find expat groups for that country or city. You'll be able to get a sense for how active and accessible the communities are based on their posting activity, and you should consider that in your decision to go there.

That's because ideally, it's best to have a balance between your expat community and your local community, but that can be difficult to create if the expat community is a little weaker—which you can gauge from Facebook or other social media. If no one's posted in a month, you either haven't found the right group or the community is just not that strong.

The reason I recommend a balance between local and expat communities is because I've seen both extremes. I've seen Americans who only want to talk to locals; they want to engage very little with other travelers. The other extreme is where people only gravitate to other Americans and barely speak to the locals. It is possible to have a good time and benefit from the experience with either extreme. However, your experience is likely to be more fulfilling if you are involved with both the local and expat communities in the areas where you live.

The challenge with creating a balanced community for yourself is that meeting expats is easy. As I said, you can find them on social media. Meeting locals can take more effort and, sometimes, patience. But I've learned some ways to do it.

For example, I play sports, and it's always easy to find

an expat community to play soccer or basketball. But you can also just go to a court or a field and find locals playing.

If you're not into sports, another good option is a language exchange. This is where locals and expats meet up to learn about each other's culture. This works really well because you'll meet locals who are already curious about your culture and want to talk to you and make friends, so that's a great starting place to get to know people. If you're in a Western country where they already speak English, you can just find groups based on specific activities or interests.

To find those groups, I love to use meetup.com. In every major city, you should be able to find some type of language exchange or a variety of shared-interest groups. For example, there are often groups for hiking, camping, or other specific hobbies. You just find the groups you're interested in that have events coming up, join the groups, and go to meet them. Meetup.com is the best for this, and Facebook groups are probably a close second.

I think travelers these days are fortunate because there are a ton of tools available for meeting people—more than there ever have been. If you want to connect with people, there is a way to do it. You just have to find the right tool. Another good website for meeting people is internations.org, which is specifically for people who are interested in networking, and you will often find longer-term expats there.

This community-building can also be part of your research process before you leave home. You can find a language exchange in your own city for the expat community of people from the country you're considering. So, for instance, you can find expats from Thailand who are living in your home city of Boston (or wherever), and you can attend the language exchange right at home. This way, you can get a chance to learn about the culture and language ahead of time.

Another reason I recommend finding groups based on common interests is that it makes it a lot easier to get to know people. If you're interacting with only a few new people every month, it can be difficult to make quality connections with people you really share common interests with. By joining a group that plays sports, or goes hiking, or does coding, or whatever it is, that shortens the distance between you and those other people. And you're much more likely to be able to make friends that way.

Facing Expat Challenges

As a traveler, the things that feel the most challenging are usually the ones that are the most mundane at home. Getting a haircut, going to the dentist, going to a doctor. We barely think about those things at home because we know exactly how the system works. But when you're abroad, accomplishing those tasks takes a lot more thought and there are more obstacles to work through. There's the language barrier, having to navigate the medical system as an expat instead of a native-born citizen, and having to figure out a different infrastructure even for things like printing a document and paying for it at a print shop.

Luckily, the best way to handle this is pretty simple: adjust your expectations. You'll be able to accomplish whatever it is you need, but it might not be as fast or as convenient as it would be at home, and maybe you won't be able to do it in exactly the same way as you were planning. Set aside more time, do more double-checking on what you'll need to get it done, and you should be fine. Ask your local friends for help—they are the experts! Remember, this was part of what you wanted out of the travel experience—to get away from your routine and encounter new things. Well, that means encountering new systems and new challenges, too.

These small challenges also mean a greater reward when you do successfully accomplish one of these small tasks. You feel great, because you just learned something new. Now, I kind of enjoy the challenge of getting a haircut from someone who doesn't speak English, using hand gestures or simple words to express what I want. And some of my worst haircuts have been from people who spoke perfect English, so there you go.

I find one of the best tools for navigating a tricky exchange, where neither of you can clearly communicate in the other's language, is to use body language. A quick laugh and a smile can lighten the situation and put people at ease, making them more willing to help you. Being a good sport, not taking yourself too seriously—those are all helpful approaches people can sense without needing language. This is so important because as a traveler who doesn't speak the local language, you often need a little extra help from people, so you need to be able to help others feel like they're on your side so they'll want to help figure out your problem with you.

Becoming an Expert Expat

In my opinion, becoming an expert expat is all about being willing and able to adapt. Some of that is preparation and some of it is in the moment. You can research local etiquette, hand gestures, how to dress, and so on ahead of time to learn the things you might not be able to figure out on your own. That way, you'll at least know what to avoid when you're there. For example, a big area for etiquette internationally is when you're visiting any kind of religious center. Whether it's a temple, church, or mosque, there will often be a specific etiquette to follow, and you can look that up ahead of time.

Observing that etiquette is about showing respect for the culture and the religion. It's not about your own personal values. You will often have to dress to cover up a bit more, and that goes for men as well as women. Temples in Thailand, for example, require men to wear shorts that cover the knee (or full-length pants, of course). This might be unfamiliar for Americans, but it's important to show respect for the religion you're visiting, and part of that respect is in looking up the expectations ahead of time and being prepared. This will also allow you to decide, "This place is too constricting, I might not enjoy my visit," and just avoid it altogether if it's going to create a problem for you.

So there's some advanced preparation, and then there's the stuff you can learn along the way, noticing the things you're doing that work and don't work, and putting some effort into adjusting to other people's expectations as you figure out what they are. It's something to be aware of as you're traveling—how others are responding to you, when people seem to open up to you or shut down—and then figuring out how to adjust to that information.

I think an important area of focus if you want to be an expat is to consider how you add value to the community. That may mean small things, like not littering and avoiding behaviors you wouldn't want to see in your home country. It could also be something bigger, like volunteering or helping locals with a project—just getting involved. Not only can this help you become part of the community, it can also help with becoming a resident if that's what you want to do. Ultimately, it just feels good to give back, and it enriches your stay. You may also hire locals to help you out, if you have the resources. It could be hiring assistants, a language teacher, a maid, or any number of others who can help you with your business or home life. I see that as giving someone a job and an income.

One way I've done this is by going out of my way to work with locals I've met who have a strong work ethic and go above and beyond. I met an Uber driver in Colombia who was more than helpful and always willing to do something extra, and he spoke great English. I learned that he had recently been let go from his job. So anytime I needed a ride, instead of calling a random Uber driver, I would call him directly and pay a little bit more because I wanted to help him specifically. I hired him as a private tour guide to show my dad around the city when he came. This man was always willing to go the extra mile, so we benefited, and we tried to give him work whenever we could, so it was a win-win. Looking for ways to help out, whether it's certain individuals or a whole community, I think is really important for becoming a good expat.

ROMANIA

Crossing Your T's and Dotting Your I's

Disclaimer: I am not a financial advisor, and this is not financial advice. In this section, I'll share some of my personal experience and the lessons I've learned about handling money and taxes while working abroad. One more time, for those in the back: this does not constitute legal or financial advice.

The first thing I want to mention is the foreign earned income exclusion (FEIE). As I've mentioned, I work for a US company and I live in Colombia. Since I work for a company in the United States, I'm technically a tourist whenever I visit a country or live somewhere else. I'm not employed within that country, which means I don't have "foreign" income. The FEIE is a tax benefit that allows you to reduce your taxable income *significantly* if you live outside of the States for 330 days out of the year (any twelve-month period). As of 2018, that benefit is for up to US$104,000 in income, and it's indexed for inflation for subsequent years. At that income level, you save about $20,000 in taxes you would otherwise have to pay. Some of my friends have explained this to me as "getting paid $20,000 a year to not live in America," which sounds really funny. But the idea is, if you're really living outside of America, you're not using any American infrastructure or resources, so why should you have to pay the taxes that pay for them? And because I don't have Colombian income, I don't have to pay income tax in Colombia. I also don't have any assets or a bank account based in Colombia.

Since I want to use this tax benefit, I watch how many days I spend in the States to make sure I don't go over the limit, and I leave a buffer in case of emergencies. I actually maintain a spreadsheet to track my visa days for my stay in Colombia as well as days in the United States, because it's an extremely important detail. If I go over on my Colombia visa days, I pay a fine; and if I go over on my days in America, I have to pay taxes. One way I try to avoid this is by spending some time traveling in a third location with family and friends (outside of Colombia and the United States).

If you are working in another country and earning foreign income, you have to declare it and pay taxes on it in that country. I had to do that for my income in Australia and New Zealand because I was working for local companies in those countries. It can get a little complicated, but I think those particular countries have a pretty good system for helping people figure out what they owe and pay it. It does help to hire an expert, and it is what a lot of people do. But the basic system is pretty easy to understand.

In Australia and New Zealand, you get a tax number when you register with the government (which you can do online), and you give that to your employer. They start deducting taxes from your paycheck—and it's a lot of tax in those countries. Then, if you make less than a certain income, you get a refund at the end of the year. It can come to $5,000 or $6,000, which is probably a lot more than tax refunds in the United States. You may not be eligible for the refund if you've earned more than a certain amount of money, but I think most travelers would be eligible for something. In both countries, you can file your taxes with an online platform—you check a few boxes, enter your information, and have the tax refund sent directly to your bank account.

☐   RWANDA

Bank accounts in general are something you'll need to research if you want to be a longer-term expat and work in the country. Opening a bank account typically isn't very difficult; you just need some documents—ID and so on. Banks want your money, so there will always be a way to navigate whatever process they have and open an account, even if they require extra security considerations or whatever it may be. If you don't need a local bank account because you're working remotely, then there isn't much point in opening one unless there are specific tax incentives available. Because there are so many variables, this is a topic you will need to research with your specific situation in mind.

Final Thoughts on the Expat Life

Personally, once I feel like an expat in a location, that's where I experience the real "freedom" that people talk about finding with travel. I can go anywhere around the world and start a life. One advantage to being born in America is having the opportunity to go and work in other countries and put roots down almost anywhere. Only a small percentage of countries in the world allow their citizens to have that right. So I think it's really important to take advantage of this freedom that we have—to go and experience other countries.

Once you've experienced this for yourself—moving somewhere and just making a go of it—it can become almost addictive. It's just so fulfilling, provides such a sense of accomplishment, and allows you to set up your life and work in ways you never could in the United States.

In the next chapter, I'll discuss all my tried-and-true practical tips for traveling, from how to pack to what credit cards are best, what items and gear I carry, and how to handle your important documentation on the go.

CHAPTER 6:

TRAVEL TIPS

Intro

I've been traveling full time since 2011, so for almost eight years now, and part time for two or three years before that. That's almost ten years! As another way of looking at it, through various rewards programs, I've earned over a million travel miles (a.k.a. frequent flyer miles). I've also visited more than seventy countries—and counting. In that time, I've learned many tools and tricks for traveling. Some I picked up from other travelers, some I figured out for myself, and some I definitely learned the hard way. In this chapter, I'll tell you everything I know about how to travel in a way that will avoid headaches and let you get the most out of your trip.

Overall, the theme of this chapter is flexibility. Whether it's the items you pack, or the dates for your trip, or the credit cards you use (and lose …), plans need to be flexible, items need to be versatile, and you should always have a backup plan. In this chapter I'll show you how to handle your money, pack light, and leave space for the unexpected.

For example: I was traveling in Patagonia and staying in a small town. I had one work task to do while I was traveling: a business call on Monday. But when we got to the town, we found that there was no cell network and no Wi-Fi connection at all—I couldn't dial in! The call wasn't for a few days, so we stayed for a bit and then cut our trip short by a day and went back to a larger town where there was cellular access. I had built enough leeway into our travel plans that we were able to do that pretty easily, whereas if I had created a highly structured itinerary for the trip, with nonrefundable reservations and tickets, I probably would have had to cancel something and lost money.

This chapter is all about how to travel long term in a way that leaves you open and able to act on whatever random opportunities (or obstacles) may come up.

Banking, Credit Cards, Spending

This first section deals with money, because some of these tips are things that need to be set up before your departure. Other tips concern long-term arrangements, like the best credit cards and American banks to use. Others are situations you need to be prepared for as soon as you land, like how to handle your important cards and documents.

My first tip related to banking is: *Make sure to tell your bank(s) that you're going to be traveling.* The number one problem travelers run into when they land in another country is that they go to an ATM and their card gets denied because the bank blocked it, thinking the card has been stolen. The situation becomes even more frustrating when you call them to correct the error and they can't immediately fix it because the system is blocking it for some reason. This can leave you stranded without cash for a few days while it all gets sorted out, which can be a serious problem. All this can be avoided with one phone call to your banks and credit card providers, telling them where you're going—before you leave home.

You should also research the country you're planning on going to, in advance, to figure out:

- The exchange rate

- The cost of living

- Widely accepted forms of payment (i.e., credit cards or cash)

Ideally, you'd like to get a favorable exchange rate where your American dollar will go further in the country, which is the case for most of Latin America and southeast Asia. However, in more developed countries like the United Kingdom and throughout Europe, the local currency is worth more than American dollars, so things will be relatively expensive. This is good information to have in your planning phase, while you're figuring out how much money you'll need.

When traveling, as much as I try to use credit cards because of the rewards and benefits you can get, cash is still king in most of the world, and you tend to need it for emergencies or when you're in particularly remote locations. I recommend carrying at least $200–300 in US dollars as a reserve.

So when you arrive, you'll want to get some cash as soon as possible. I would recommend heading straight to an ATM to withdraw money instead of going to an exchange. For one thing, the exchange rate may not be favorable at the airport and you could get ripped off. Whatever cash you're already carrying, you'll want to keep for emergencies. You'll want to have more cash for walking around, which is another lesson I learned on my travels.

I was in Tokyo, traveling from the airport to my friend's house, and I had to make a number of transfers on different trains along the way, buying a new ticket each time. The ticket machines only accepted cash. So I bought my first train ticket, spending all the Japanese yen I had on me. At the next transfer point, I needed to buy another ticket, but they wouldn't take my card, so I went looking for an ATM. I found two or three, but none of them would take my debit card. Travelers in Japan can't use just any ATM—you have to find an international ATM, and there wasn't one close to where I was.

I finally found a currency exchange, and I exchanged the four different currencies I had on me to get enough yen for my next train ticket. I don't know what I would have done if I hadn't been able to scrounge together enough cash for the ticket.

That experience taught me to always carry a fair amount of "emergency cash," preferably in US dollars; if not dollars, then euros, and if not euros, then pound sterling.

Ideally, you've withdrawn cash at the airport, so you have local currency right away. If the ATM at the airport isn't working for some reason, you can use the cash you have on hand to get to the hotel, and then ask the hotel staff where you can find the closest international ATM. Another benefit to withdrawing cash with an ATM is that if you have a travel credit card, you'll get the best exchange rate and no fee, as opposed to a currency exchange that may give you a bad rate and will definitely charge a fee.

Another situation to avoid is having only one means of accessing cash, and I have a story about that, too.

I was in Thailand one night, trying to withdraw cash from my bank. I found an ATM and had just put my debit card into the machine, and the power went out in the whole city. On the island of Thailand most transactions are cash based, so I panicked, thinking the machine had eaten my debit card. Imagine being on a Thai island with very little access, and your only source of cash is potentially locked inside an ATM. That was definitely an "oh, shit" moment.

Fortunately, the power came back on a few minutes later, and my card came back out. But that incident showed me exactly how vulnerable I was, with only one debit card as my sole means of accessing cash in that country. As the saying goes, you don't want to have all your eggs in one basket. Since then, I make sure I have multiple debit cards that I can use to get cash, I never carry just one wallet that has everything in it, and I don't carry my important documents on me at all once I get settled in. Anything you carry with you is a lot more likely to get lost than items that are stationary in one place. And that's not even accounting for the possibilities of theft.

Once I've arrived in a location, I secure my passport, debit cards, and important documents, either in a safe (if I'm at a hotel) or hidden in my luggage. I have photos of my credit cards and passports (including the ID page and entry stamp), proof of insurance coverage, photo ID, and anything else I deem important. Those photos are saved in a secure note, and on the cloud, and locally on my phone, and as encrypted PDFs in my email. On a side note, it's very easy to find apps that will convert a picture to a PDF right from your phone, and then you just set up the security options on the PDF so it's password protected.

I store these security documents in multiple locations, because you never know what might happen—your phone could break, you might not have internet access at the moment that you need to show something—there are a lot of possibilities. So it's important to be prepared by backing up your documents with multiple copies stored in different locations.

Anything I carry on me is stuff that I'm okay with losing—a credit card that I can cancel and/or have multiples of; my ID, which is not a driver's license—it's a global entry card; enough cash for the day or the week, but not so much that it would be a disaster if I lost it. So my whole wallet could get lost or stolen, and my plans for the day would barely change.

Regarding other kinds of payment methods while traveling, I do not use traveler's checks—and I don't recommend them. They're outdated and don't offer any of the benefits or security of a credit card. I believe credit cards are the best way to go. If you're young and don't have your own credit, you can usually be added as an authorized user on your parent's credit cards. This won't help you build much of a credit history, because the account is still in your parent's name, but it will at least give you access to a credit card.

When you travel with so many important cards and documents, you've got to be cautious about how you use them to avoid scams and fraud. When I use my debit card to get cash, I use ATMs inside banks to avoid getting my card skimmed. ATMs on the street can be sketchy, but banks check their ATMs regularly (some check multiple times every day) to make sure there are no card-skimming devices, so that's the way I roll. I prefer to carry credit cards over debit cards because it's a lot easier to cancel and replace a credit card than a debit card, and you have better protection from fraudulent transactions. You can also protect yourself by setting withdrawal limits on your debit card and fraud alerts for your credit cards so you'll be notified of any unusual activity.

Whether you plan on working in the country or not, you will need to find a way to avoid paying international fees on every transaction, because that's what will happen by default. Whether it's your credit card or debit card, there is often a percentage fee per transaction, and it adds up. I suggest Charles Schwab for a debit account, since they reimburse all ATM fees every month (foreign and domestic). In Colombia, it's $3 or $4 for each ATM withdrawal, so to have that reimbursed monthly is significant. I save around $500 a year in ATM fees by using this service.

A major tip is to set up your credit cards, banking, and travel so that every dollar you spend earns you rewards, whether it's points or some other benefit. I pay by card whenever I can for this reason. Make sure to sign up for frequent flyer programs with the airlines you use; I find you get treated a little bit better, and the systems just seem to work better if you're a member. It's free to sign up, and even if you don't fly with that airline a lot, it's a great idea to sign up so you can collect miles when you do use it. You can keep an eye out for promotions where you earn double or triple miles and time your travel accordingly to earn major bonus points.

There is also a way to use credit cards strategically, to get sign-up bonuses once you spend a certain amount, along with the usual benefits. It's called "credit card hacking," but there's nothing illegal or shifty about it. You just have to be able to justify whatever amount of spending you have to do to get the bonus—which is typically worth anywhere from $500 to $1,000. But if you're smart about spending and optimizing the bonus points, they can be worth two or three times that value.

If you want the sign-up bonuses but don't think you'll spend the amount to get it, what some people do is sign up for a prepaid Visa gift card and put $3,000 on it, or whatever is needed to get the sign-up bonus. That way, the money will still be available and you can spend it, but it goes toward your spending for the sign-up bonus. I don't do this because I spend enough normally, and I'm not sure I would recommend it, as prepaid gift cards often come with a lot of limits and conditions. You would need to read the fine print carefully to make sure you understand what you're getting into. I would recommend sticking with whatever promotions you can access through your normal spending—it's just one less thing to think about.

As an example, my two day-to-day credit cards are the American Express (AmEx) Platinum and the Chase Sapphire Reserve. They both provide a large sign-up bonus and other incentives that are worth about $200–300 per year. Essentially, they either reimburse more than what I spend on travel, or they reward that spending somehow. Also, they both have great travel protections, extended warranties, access to airport lounges, and priority passes for air travel. The AmEx Platinum card gives me access to The Centurion Lounge—which is one of the nicest lounges I've been to—it offers free manicures and massages, a full buffet, and top-shelf alcohol. I travel through Miami a lot, and this system works well for me because one of my credit cards gives me a free meal in one of the Miami restaurants, while the other gives me access to the airport lounge where I can rest, eat, and get some work done.

These credit cards, since they're geared for travel expenses, also give me access to Global Entry, which is a faster way of getting through the security line for flights entering the United States; you go to a Global Entry kiosk, put in your information, and get through the line in no time. When departing the US, there's TSA precheck, which is also faster—no pulling things out of your bag, no taking off your shoes. That's perfect for me because of how much I travel. When you're evaluating credit cards, make sure you look for the benefits that you will actually use and that are targeted for your situation.

☐   SINGAPORE

In general, people tend to be a little afraid of opening new credit card accounts because they're concerned it will negatively affect their credit score, but I've had more than ten at different times as a traveler and maintained a credit score above 800. You just need to make sure you're paying off the balances each month and not spending more than you earn. And I don't open credit cards and then close them quickly (that *is* bad for your credit score). I keep them open. If I am not using a credit card anymore and it's not worth the annual fee, I don't close the account, I just downgrade to a card without an annual fee. That way, the account stays open and I continue building my credit history. If you are considering credit card hacking, I'd recommend starting with one or two; walk before you run. Bit by bit, you'll build up your own system.

If you're planning to send or receive money while traveling, there are a lot of options. I recommend PayPal or TransferWise, which are the easiest ways to transfer money, and they're also relatively secure. Both PayPal and TransferWise are good options for this. If you're with a big bank, like Citibank, you can often transfer money from one Citibank account to another international location for free. I also recommend Charles Schwab because their checking accounts are linked right to their investor accounts, so you can conduct investment strategies right from your checking account.

When it comes to making hotel reservations or booking flights, try to keep the schedule flexible, even if it means paying more. If you want to travel to Europe during peak season, you may think, "Okay, I need to book my hotel way in advance or it'll all get booked up." That's true, but you can still maintain your flexibility with a refundable booking.

They typically cost a little more, but they'll let you cancel with just a few days' notice. I do this all the time, even if I feel my plans are completely set in stone, because you just never know what might come up. And this is not just in case of emergencies but also in case of something awesome happening. What if you love a city and you want to stay a few more days, or you hear about some cool detour or landmark you want to go see, or meet a fun group of people you want to travel with?

This happened to me a lot when I was traveling solo, so I started making space for unexpected plans. I would book the first night of accommodations in a city, and then see where things would go; maybe I'd meet some new people and want to extend my booking, or maybe those people would be going somewhere else in a few days and they'd invite me along. Being able to take advantage of opportunities like that is what allows you to make friends while traveling. If you only stick to your itinerary, and all your plans are fixed and payments nonrefundable, it's harder to benefit from those random opportunities to travel with others and make friends.

That's what I mean about being flexible; it's not just about being spontaneous in the moment but also making space in your arrangements for the unexpected to happen. Booking the reservation or flight that lets you change the dates, scheduling accommodations for just a few days even though you're planning to stay longer, making sure your travel arrangements are refundable whenever possible—those things will set you up to be able to benefit from whatever might come up while you're traveling.

Travel Insurance

The major tip that I have for travel insurance is: read your policy to make sure you're covered in whatever country you're going to—and make sure you know *what* is covered. If you have insurance in the United States, check to make sure it will cover you when you're abroad. If not, I highly recommend getting travel insurance that will cover *all* your travel destinations.

You will typically be required to have travel and medical insurance to get a visa. Even if it's not a requirement, I have it anyway, and I think it's worth getting. It's not uncommon for travelers to get injured while hiking in a remote area, for example, and to need a helicopter to airlift them from the mountains to a hospital. Insurance will cover that kind of thing—and without it, you could owe $200,000 or something crazy like that.

For international insurance, I recommend World Nomads, which costs around $1,000 a year and covers you in almost every country. World Nomads also covers electronics, which is a big deal if your nice camera or laptop gets damaged. I was on a ship with crazy high waves and my camera got splashed and had water damage. It was covered. I did have to provide documentation showing that I was on the ship, flight receipts to show I was in the country, and a receipt for the camera purchase, but in the end, it was worth it. This would also cover laptop theft if you're working from a café or something, which is critical if you're a remote worker and your laptop is your means of making money. If you're going to be staying in one place, it might make sense to look at local insurance options and figure out if that would work better for you.

The Thai medical system, for example, is inexpensive and offers exceptional value. You can have procedures performed in Thailand, even routine things like a root canal, for way cheaper, even outside of insurance coverage.

Another tip for staying safe while traveling: when you're researching countries, and even before your departure, keep an eye on the news. It's a good idea to register for the US government program called the Smart Traveler Enrollment Program (STEP). This is a way to sort of register yourself with the nearest US embassy when you're traveling. You'll receive alerts in case of an emergency or evacuation, and it will make it easier for your family to reach you if something happens back home. Sometimes there will be alerts that don't apply to you, and I wouldn't recommend avoiding a country just because there's a STEP alert out, but it can be a useful system in case of an emergency.

SOMALIA

Transportation

I get asked all the time about finding cheap flights. My number one tip is: be flexible with travel dates. There are lots of new flight services (like Scott's Cheap Flights) that will send you flight deals once you specify a certain destination. To take advantage of these services, you just decide where you're going to travel for the next few months and set alerts for those months to see what the lowest prices are. Google Flights is great for this. Just switch to the monthly view while searching, and that will let you see where you can save $300 just by leaving on a different day. This strategy is sort of the reverse of a conventional booking system, which prompts you to enter the dates first, and then book the flight. With this tip, you enter the flight details first, and then look at dates. And of course, when you do purchase your airline tickets, still try to keep your options open for canceling or changing the dates.

Another tip is to use alternative airports—the ones nearby that are less used than the major city airport. For example, fly into New Jersey instead of New York City. Or if Chicago is your destination, fly in and out of Midway Airport instead of O'Hare. It might mean taking a connecting flight or a forty-five-minute drive, but it could save you hundreds of dollars.

As far as getting around once you reach your destination, I think Uber is the way to go. They're in a lot of places around the world and they have the lowest rates and the best interface, so I highly recommend them for transportation around the city. Another option, particularly in Europe or Asia, is the local transportation, which is typically very affordable. There is usually an app for navigating the buses and trains, so make sure you find that app and maybe download it ahead of time.

Resources

These are some specific tools and apps that I use a lot. They're mostly applicable across different countries and can help save you some money—and headaches.

- *Project Fi (SIM card that can be used in 180 countries)*: This is a service run by Google, which allows you to use the local cellular service. It costs $20 per month, and you have the option to pick whichever local network you want to use. You can use your current SIM card, connect to any local network, and just pay for the data you use. Right now, the data fee is about $10 per gig, with a max of $80, so sometimes if I'm in an area where the Wi-Fi is terrible, I will just use data through Project Fi for the whole time, because I know I won't pay more than $80.

- *Google Translate*: This is probably the best translation app because it's been using machine learning to develop over time. There is a really useful feature in Google Translate where you can translate a restaurant menu just by pointing your phone camera at it (from within the app), and on your screen it will show the translated menu. It's almost like an augmented-reality type of experience—really cool and very useful.

- *TripIt*: This is an app that syncs with my email. I use it to coordinate all my trip dates and logistics. Anytime I make a booking or a reservation, it pulls that information and displays it in an organized, chronological way,

with booking numbers and details and everything.
And it's completely free.

- *Google Maps offline maps*: This feature lets you download a map offline for when you're traveling in an area where you won't have internet access. I recommend doing this as much as possible because it's just one more way of protecting yourself if something unexpected happens. On a side note, GPS doesn't require an internet connection—it uses satellites. So you can download a map when you have internet access, pull up the map when you're somewhere without internet, and still use GPS to navigate. It won't be quite as accurate, but it still works. This feature also allows you to show a picture of your destination and its address on the offline map to cab drivers, or anyone you ask for directions. This can make it a lot easier to find your way around if you're somewhere where you don't speak the language.

- *Currency converters*: XE has a great app that lets you look at ten different currencies. I use this mostly for withdrawing cash, as it helps you easily figure out how much to withdraw in the local currency.

- *TripAdvisor*: You can download locations and view them offline, and it helps you figure out the best restaurants and things in the area.

- Ask a local: This isn't an app—it's just a tip. As important as it is to do your research ahead of time, there are some things that a local will know best, so don't be afraid to ask around if you want to get recommendations for where to eat or fun places to go. This is how you find out about the things you wouldn't know just from looking online, and it's a great way to build some spontaneity into your trip.

Networking

One of the themes of this book is how important it is to network, keep in touch with friends and acquaintances, and nurture those relationships. The way I see it, networking is the process of taking the friendships and acquaintances you already have and turning them into something more—almost into a partnership, where they're engaged in helping you and you're engaged in helping them.

To get started with networking, you can attend actual networking events that are just full of people looking to make meaningful connections. You'll meet a ton of people in a short time. Much like speed dating, you have to figure out who you're interested in, either for a friendship or a work connection, and contact them later to follow up. Go for coffee or lunch, or any activity they would be interested in, and just keep nurturing that relationship. You never know where it could lead.

You should also consider what platform is best for each relationship. I find emails are the most professional, while Facebook is convenient for messaging and can also help keep you top of mind for contacts you don't talk to all the time—as long as you're comfortable with these contacts seeing your posts. If not, there are a variety of privacy restrictions or contact groupings you can use to control what your network contacts see. Similarly, LinkedIn is great for messaging and is more of a professional environment. You can also share content that's specific to your industry, that wouldn't seem interesting on Facebook but can be part of your branding on LinkedIn.

A truly useful tip for networking, especially if you travel, is to *back up your contacts*. It's very easy to do and can be done for your Facebook contacts, email contacts, phone numbers, etc. Then you'll never have to be that person posting online telling everyone you lost your phone.

If you do have network contacts on Facebook, you'll also be able to see what city they're in. In Facebook, you can search "friends in Tokyo" and it will show you everyone you know on Facebook who lives in Tokyo. That is immensely helpful when you're in a new city. It's probably the fastest way to figure out if you know anyone, and I always find it shows me people I wouldn't have thought of but am happy to reach out to once I know they're nearby. So it can be a great way of strengthening those "warm" contacts—people you know indirectly or not very well.

Phone and Internet

My biggest tip in terms of phones is to get an unlocked phone. Having an unlocked phone allows you to travel to a bunch of different locations and just have a phone that works. Unlocked phones work in almost every country. The iPhone X, which I have, works with both CDMA and GSM. That means it will work on every type of carrier worldwide. Having an unlocked phone is the best way to go because it will work on both of the common cellular bandwidths. Another way to use your phone in a new country is to buy a local SIM card and just put it in your phone.

Another helpful tip is to use airplane mode on your phone as much as possible. Your phone will charge much faster and keep its charge longer. You won't be able to receive calls, but you'll still be able to browse using Wi-Fi. I highly recommend this practice to keep your precious battery charged for as long as you can.

Packing Tips

TRAVELING LIGHT

I am a big believer in traveling with one carry-on bag. It might take some getting used to, but it is a nice feeling to have everything you need on you, ready to go. With one bag, you're a lot more mobile and flexible. You don't have to wait around baggage claim in airports or worry about your luggage getting lost or put on the wrong plane. It makes me feel more agile and lighter, and more in control.

I pack for seven to ten days, regardless of how long I'm going to stay; it just means I'll need to do laundry about every ten days. For some reason, maybe it's an American thing, we don't tend to think of doing laundry when we travel. If we're going somewhere for twenty-one days, we want to take twenty-one days' worth of everything. But laundry facilities are fairly accessible overseas. In Asia, there are really inexpensive services that will pick up your laundry, wash it, fold it, and bring it back to you, which is awesome. Depending on where you're traveling, it may be a matter of planning for an Airbnb that has a washer and dryer.

To keep your packed items to a minimum, buy whatever you can locally or arrange to have it wherever you're staying. Items like replacement charger cables, blow dryers, toothpaste, and shampoo can be bought once you arrive or may be supplied at your accommodations, and it will save a lot of money and space in your luggage. I also wouldn't recommend trying to take your $200 blow dryer or hair straightener to Europe anyway, because the converter could ruin it. Just find a store once you arrive and pick up whatever personal items you need.

I identify as a minimalist in terms of packing and having "stuff." I have the mentality that if I buy another article of clothing, I need to give something up. Shoes are a bit more of a struggle; I have a pair of compact running shoes that squish down for easy packing and a pair of Sperrys (boat shoes) I can kind of dress up or dress down (and I don't need to wear socks with them). I also have a nice pair of Cole Haan dress shoes that I wear with jeans for more "business casual" situations. I enjoy being able to go to a nice bar or restaurant when I'm in a city, so I need to be able to dress for that. It's a personal preference, but it's important to me as part of the travel experience.

I basically have what's called a "capsule closet." My wardrobe consists of a few items of clothing that can be worn in a variety of combinations to cover just about every situation (daytime, evening, casual, and business casual), in colors that coordinate—I mostly stick with solid tones instead of patterns—and each item being as versatile as possible.

Here is the list of all the clothing I own:

- 1 x Khaki shorts

- 2 x Nike Dri-FIT shorts

- 7 x Under Armour Boxerjocks

- 3 x V-neck T-shirts

- 2 x Tank tops

- 1 x Nike Dri-FIT gym shirt

- 2 x Button-downs

- 3 x Shoes (Sperrys, Cole Haans, and Nike Free RNs)

- 3 x Socks (Nike socks)

- 1 x Burberry polo

- 1 x Jeans (7 For All Mankind)

- 1 x Travel jacket

If you're like me and enjoy going out to upscale places, you'll love this tip for how to deal with the wrinkles in all your rolled-up shirts: I use Wrinkle Release, a spray that you apply to your clothes to get the wrinkles out. It comes in a travel size, which of course makes it great for traveling. Another way to deal with wrinkles is to hang up your clothes in the bathroom while you're having a hot shower—the steam will help loosen up the wrinkles.

I've heard (a lot!) that women need to pack more stuff than men do, but this isn't necessarily true. My girlfriend and I traveled through Panama for a month, and she had just one small backpack—almost half the size of mine. She packed a pair of flats she could wear with anything, a pair of gym shoes, and a few outfits. She had one top that she could wear to a formal event, to the gym, or to the beach over a swimsuit. I know it's hard to find stuff like that, but it does exist, and it makes a huge difference for packing. She did not take a blow dryer. Just saying. Women's clothing tends to be lighter and smaller as well, so it all depends on the individual.

Packing like a minimalist is also good for avoiding "decision fatigue." If you only have two shirts, you don't have to think too hard about what to wear. That's important when you're moving through new cities and countries and having to make a ton of decisions about things you never had to think about at home. Then there's the time savings. I figure I probably save a few days a year by traveling with one carry-on instead of checking my luggage. I avoid those massive check-in lines every time, because I check in online and head straight to security. This saves me so much time and unnecessary stress at the airport.

I think minimalist packing is a gradual development for some people. As a traveler, you eventually reach the point where you think, "Hey, this really isn't necessary. I always wear the same two shirts anyway." Then, if you pull out the clothing items you're not wearing, you have more room for underwear—which means less laundry. I definitely overpacked when I was starting out, and I think a lot of travelers do, until they have that "aha moment" and realize it's not worth the time and effort.

If you're new to traveling and don't feel ready for a single carry-on, try to travel with one suitcase and a carry-on. Everything valuable should be in the carry-on—electronics, medication, documents. Over time, you'll likely get to where you're using just a carry-on, like me. My carry-on bag is a backpack. It's a clamshell-loader (a highly technical backpack term), which means you can fully unzip it and pack it like a suitcase, instead of being a conventional backpack that you load from the top. I used a top-loader for years and recently moved to this clamshell-loader; it makes a big difference and is much more convenient. After careful research and testing, I now use packing cubes in my carry-on because they help compress your stuff, and I also roll up my clothing, which makes it take up less space.

You should have a photo of your luggage, and a photo of everything you've packed, stored somewhere safe (not in your luggage!) in case it ever goes missing, or if you check your bag and it gets lost, you'll need to show the airline staff what it looks like to help them find it.

When shopping for a travel bag, the main requirement is that it fits the dimensions for most airlines for a carry-on bag. I like to have a laptop compartment and a small pouch or compartment for toiletries, and a separate compartment or packing cube for my shoes. Dirty laundry goes in my shoe compartment of the bag, with clean clothes separated inside the packing cubes. A rolling suitcase could work too, as long as it's not too big.

As far as food and drinks, having a reusable water bottle is absolutely crucial. A few Clif Bars or Kind bars (or something similar) are great to have in case there's a delay or you get hungry on a bus or plane. But just carry a few—not a month's supply. Once you arrive at your destination, you can find a grocery store and pick up whatever their local version is. This is another kind of flexibility—being able to compromise on the food you're looking for. I promise you will be able to find *something* along the lines of whatever you have in mind. Every country and culture has its own comfort foods, classic dishes, and fast food, its own hot and cold beverages, snacks, and bars. It just might not look exactly like what you had in mind.

BRING RELIABLE ELECTRONICS

I like to bring a good camera (mine is a Sony RX100) to take photos and videos of my travel—that's something you'll be able to cherish for life. I also bring my laptop, of course, which is a MacBook Pro. I use my computer ten to twelve hours a day, and I use it for work, so it needs to be fast and reliable. It's a huge pain if anything goes wrong with your laptop or your phone while you're traveling, so it's definitely worth the money to buy something that won't break down or be high-maintenance.

Conclusion

In this chapter, I've tried to cover all the tips and tricks that I learned about traveling, as well as the basic principles I've developed: be flexible, have a backup plan, don't overthink your itinerary. With this, and the up-to-date posts on my website about specific travel gear (all tested by me), you should be more than ready to head off on your next long trip.

TIBET

THAILAND   ☐

CHAPTER 7:

AFTERWORD: MY FINAL THOUGHTS

O ver the course of this book, I hope I've provided enough information to prove to you that this lifestyle can work for you. Whatever your concerns were, I hope I've shown that there's a way to get past them and build a life that moves you toward your goals.

My message to you is: don't worry. Wherever you go, you won't be alone—not if you don't want to be. Practically speaking, you can start small by traveling with a group, like I did. But in general, anywhere you go, there will always be someone around who can help you. All that will change is that you might have to be the one to find them and ask for help.

If you still have misgivings, I'd say that the best cure for fear of failure is to just do it. Just book a ticket and go on a trip. Maybe a shorter trip to start, and then a longer one. As you go, you'll find resources online and locally, and you'll gain confidence as you overcome obstacles, until you quickly become a confident globe-trotter.

For example, Thailand is sort of like a mecca for digital nomads, mainly because of the low cost of living. By now, there is a local community of remote workers that's developed there, so that's a place where there are both people and resources to help you out. Chiang Mai, Thailand, is a major hub for remote work, so if you're considering working online, I would highly recommend starting there as your home base. It's affordable and has a community of digital nomads you can connect with and get advice from.

Once you get going with this work/travel life I've been talking about, you'll see for yourself the benefits I've discussed in this book. I've proven that you can earn a similar or even higher income working abroad while maintaining a better work/life balance. So you can benefit financially as well as emotionally while gaining the satisfaction of having taken on this challenge and succeeded.

One of the most important ways you'll benefit, in my opinion, is by finding countries and cultures that are a perfect fit for you. I think in the United States we tend to compromise on what we want our working life to be, maybe a little too quickly. But the advantage of traveling is that you get to see that there is a country somewhere where you *can* attain your ideal lifestyle—the one you didn't pursue because you thought it was impractical, or even impossible. And this is something you can only learn by traveling to a few different places and staying long enough (at least a few weeks) to get a feel for the culture. Once you've established—with yourself—that you can travel and move around, you'll gain a newfound ability to sample different places until you find the one that's just right, rather than staying and struggling where you are.

I sometimes hear people say they have to take a pay

cut in order to work online. They wonder why they should leave their job that pays $100,000 a year to take an online job that pays $70,000. The answer is: with the online job, they can work from a country where the cost of living is a fraction of what it is in the United States, and still save way more money. The question is not "How much money will I make?" Rather, it's "How much money will I be able to save?" or even better, "What kind of lifestyle can I afford?" Because the answers to those questions might pleasantly surprise you. To use myself as an example, I would estimate that I'm able to save about 60 percent of each paycheck rather than spending it on bills, just because I live in a much more affordable country.

The main point of this book has been to show that traveling is not reserved for people who have "the right kind of job" or are at "the right point in their lives." It can be something that supports your career, helps you increase your earning potential, and even supports your transition into another industry.

That said, it's not all about material gains; there are important emotional benefits too. Traveling will help you expand your network, try new things, and broaden your horizons. Once you start traveling, you will probably gain a new perspective on your previous office-based lifestyle. You might realize you were really living for the weekends, as compared to a life of traveling and working abroad where every day is exciting and fulfilling on its own.

My job, for example, supports a lot of training and education, so I'm continually taking marketing courses to improve my skills—that's in addition to the MBA I completed in South Korea. My industry is constantly changing and growing and getting more interesting, and I get to engage with that through learning. So through traveling abroad, I found a job that keeps my skills fresh and allows me to engage with new developments in my field. This lifestyle also allows me to develop other skills, like photography and writing, which are really fulfilling, and I have the time to develop them and create things like my website. So the remote work really supports my whole life, not just my career aspirations.

I'm positive that I wouldn't have been able to build a life like this if I had focused on finding a job in a traditional office setting. By taking up remote work, I achieved independence and freedom, and I really want to help others get there—even faster than I did.

The thing is, I'm not the only person out there who wants to help others. I've found that in the community of remote workers and travelers, people are really open to helping others. I think we all feel extremely fortunate to have found the opportunities we did, and there's a feeling of wanting to help others get there, too. So once you find a community of travelers or expats, I think you'll find it's easy to start making connections and building friendships, because the community is so open to that.

What this means for you is that there are networking opportunities out there, where networking is not something onerous and it's not about using people. Instead, it's about finding mentorship in this community. You can start by noticing the people who are where you'd like to be in five years or so, and reaching out to them. It can be a little scary to put yourself out there like that, but as I said, you will probably find that they are ready and willing to help you. You just need to be able to learn and listen.

I find that networking among travelers is highly

rewarding because you can quickly expand your connections all over the world, and you get exposure to other cultures and ways of thinking at the same time. You can find a mentor from another country who can teach you so much, not only professionally but about perspectives on life and work that you might not have been exposed to before.

From Novice to Expert

You might be thinking, "Well, this sounds great, but I've never even been on an international flight, flown by myself, or planned my own travel before, so I still don't know if I can do this."

Is that you? The truth is that you can get started anytime you want just by finding someone you know who is an experienced traveler or works for a travel agency or something like that, and learning a few tips from them. (Starting to talk about your dream of travel with others will also make it more concrete in your own mind and more likely that you will actually do it.)

Take me for example, at eighteen, on my first international flight. Before that, I had mostly traveled around the United States by car. That was also my very first time on a plane. Luckily for me, I was traveling with other people. I didn't even know about checking in for my flight, the security line, any of it. I didn't know what to do once you land in a foreign country. All I had was my dad and my brother with me, and an interest in learning more about travel.

At that point in my life, I was headed for some type of corporate job. I didn't know exactly what kind, but I had in mind the usual nine-to-five daily grind—the kind of "real job" that would advance my career.

Fast-forward to now: I zip through airport lines, navigate menus in foreign languages, and carry just one backpack with everything I own (instead of being the guy with too much luggage for a short trip—which I also did, at first).

Every day, I get to wake up naturally instead of having

an alarm go off. I do a few hours of work in the morning on my laptop (at my desk or at a coworking space), go to the gym, and then I have a chef who makes me lunch. Then it's back to work, or maybe spend some time in the sauna or pool, or maybe get a coffee from a nearby coffee shop. Dinner could be from the chef at home, or I might go out with friends.

My daily life is a combination of work and travel. I pick my own hours, and my job just requires me to get the work done—not to put in "face time" at an office. So I can plan extended trips to Europe, or anywhere else, and I can flex my job around that, which I think is awesome. I have a much more balanced approach to life and work than what I ever dreamed I could achieve at eighteen.

I'd like to end by strongly encouraging you to take advantage of some (or all) of the opportunities I've out-lined: studying abroad, interning abroad, working abroad, and working remotely. As I've shown, there are tools and programs you can use to do this—so while it may seem unfamiliar at first, it's really not difficult. There are struc-tured ways to travel and resources at your disposal, espe-cially as a student.

As Americans, we have a lot of freedom to travel and work internationally (through the working holiday program, for example), which people from many other countries don't have. And I think you're doing yourself a disservice if you don't at least look into these opportunities and give it a shot. There is so much we can learn from other countries, and it can only make us better as people if we experience new things and bring home some of what we've learned.

So, please, find a working holiday program, find a study

abroad course at your university, find some friends to visit overseas—just find a way to get started on your work/travel journey. I promise it'll be worth it.

Want Some Help?

This book is intended to show people what's possible with traveling and working abroad, but like I said, that doesn't mean you have to do it all on your own. I'll help. If you'd like a consultation (I won't charge you anything for it!), just visit my website at globalcareerbook.com/talk and enter the country name "Zambia" to access the portal, since this is an exclusive offer for readers. The consultation can cover anything you want, from finding work overseas to travel tips to the nomad life, etc. You can also contact me directly via email at mike@globalcareerbook.com.

**INSPIRATION AND IDEAS
TO HELP YOU BEGIN:**

"THE WORLD IS A BOOK, AND THOSE WHO DO NOT TRAVEL READ ONLY A PAGE."

SAINT AUGUSTINE

UNITED ARAB EMIRATES

"A JOURNEY IS BEST MEASURED IN FRIENDS RATHER THAN MILES."

TIM CAHILL

"DO NOT FOLLOW WHERE THE PATH MAY LEAD. GO INSTEAD WHERE THERE IS NO PATH AND LEAVE A TRAIL."

RALPH WALDO EMERSON

UGANDA

MINIMALIST PACKING LIST (WARM WEATHER)

☐ Pair of Casual shorts
☐ Sport shorts (double as swimsuit)
☐ Underwear
☐ Casual T-shirts
☐ Gym Shirts
☐ Button-downs or nice tops
☐ Shoes (casual, formal, gym)
☐ Socks
☐ Jeans
☐ Travel jacket
☐ Passport
☐ Digital Camera
☐ Headphones
☐ Laptop
☐ Charging Cables
☐ Pen
☐ Wallet and Cash
☐ Toothbrush & Toothpaste*
☐ Deodorant*
☐ Sunscreen*

*Don't overpack too many toiletries, you can purchase everything else overseas

"ONCE A YEAR, GO SOMEPLACE YOU HAVE NEVER BEEN BEFORE."

DALAI LAMA

"THE BEST EDUCATION I HAVE EVER RECEIVED WAS THROUGH TRAVEL."

LISA LING

"TRAVEL IS FATAL TO PREJUDICE, BIGOTRY, AND NARROW-MINDEDNESS, AND MANY OF OUR PEOPLE NEED IT SORELY ON THESE ACCOUNTS. BROAD, WHOLESOME, CHARITABLE VIEWS OF MEN AND THINGS CANNOT BE ACQUIRED BY VEGETATING IN ONE LITTLE CORNER OF THE EARTH ALL ONE'S LIFETIME."

MARK TWAIN

VANUATU

YOUR BUCKET LIST

Here is where you can create a list of things you'd like to do before you die, like taking a helicopter ride over the Grand Canyon or snorkeling the Great Barrier Reef in Australia. Think big!

1. _____

2. _____

3. _____

4. _____

5. _____

6. _____

7. _____

8. _____

9. _____

10. _____

11. _____

12. _____

13. _____

14. _____

15. _____

16. _____

17. _____

18. _____

19. _____

20. _____

21. _____

22. _____

23. _____

24. _____

☐   VENEZUELA

VIETNAM   □

RESOURCES

I've compiled a list of some resources that will be extremely useful on your journey of working and traveling all around the world. The resources range from job boards to a custom-built tool that tells you exactly what visa you need for visiting other countries! In addition to this, I will be keeping all the resources updated on a regular basis since new information and changes are always happening.

- globalcareerbook.com/visas

  Finding out information about work and travel visas is a nightmare. The information is scattered all across the internet, and a lot of times, it's outdated or wrong. I've created a free tool to help show you exactly what visa you need when visiting a foreign country.

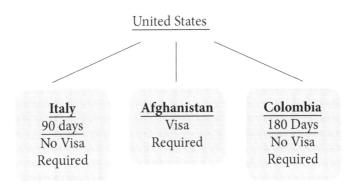

United States

Italy	Afghanistan	Colombia
90 days	Visa	180 Days
No Visa	Required	No Visa
Required		Required

- globalcareerbook.com/whv

Working holiday visas (WHV) are the easiest and best way to work and travel. I've put together an extensive page detailing everything you need to know about working holiday visas and how to start the process.

1. ———   New Zealand

2. ———   Australia

3. ———   Ireland

4. ———   South Korea

5. ———   Singapore

YEMEN   □

- globalcareer.com/jobs

  Are you interested in finding a remote, online, or international job? Then this is the best place to start! I've created a job board full of remote and international jobs, so you can start an international career from the comfort of your laptop.

- globalcareerbook.com/talk

If you are wanting to start a global career, then I would love to speak with you. This free consultation offer is only available for readers, so make sure to input the country code "Zambia." I look forward to chatting about international work, travel, and anything in between!

POTENTIAL TALKING POINTS

- ☐ Travel Tips and Tricks
- ☐ Working Overseas
- ☐ Career Advice
- ☐ Creating a Perfect Travel Itinerary
- ☐ Finding Cheap Flights
- ☐ Budgeting for a trip

P.S. If you have any questions about work or travel, feel free to email me at mike@globalcareerbook.com.